Dyslexia and Inclusion

Classroom Approaches
for Assessment, Teaching
and Learning

Gavin Reid

 David Fulton Publishers

David Fulton Publishers Ltd
The Chiswick Centre, 414 Chiswick High Road, London W4 5TF

www.fultonpublishers.co.uk

First published in Great Britain by David Fulton Publishers in association with the
National Association for Special Educational Needs (NASEN)

NASEN is a registered charity no. 1007023.

David Fulton Publishers is a division of Granada Learning Limited, part of ITV plc.

British Library Cataloguing in Publication Data
A catalogue record for this book is available from the British Library.

ISBN: 1 84312 361 4

Designed and typeset by Kenneth Burnley, Wirral, Cheshire
Printed and bound in Great Britain

Contents

Contents

Preface

The purpose of this book is to provide the class teacher with an understanding of dyslexia and to offer some specific and practical approaches for assessment, teaching and learning. The book aims to highlight how the needs of children with dyslexia can be met within the curriculum and within the mainstream classroom. The key theme of the book suggests that intervention for dyslexic children should focus on the barriers to learning, and the most prominent of these may be aspects of the curriculum and how the curriculum is presented. That is not to say that identifying cognitive difficulties are not important. They are, as these can help to inform the teacher of the potential difficulties that can be experienced by children with dyslexia. But it is crucial that the literacy and cognitive difficulties usually associated with dyslexia should not dictate classroom approaches, or curriculum content. The key is to be pro-active and to anticipate the type of difficulties that can be experienced, and to ensure that through carefully prepared IEPs (individual education plans), insightful use of resources and, above all, through differentiation and learning styles, that the curriculum can be accessed by all dyslexic children.

In order for this to be effective teachers need to have an understanding of dyslexia and to be aware of criteria that can be used for identification and assessment. This is, therefore, covered in Chapter 1 of this book. Class teachers, it is suggested here, have the responsibility for identifying and ensuring that the needs of dyslexic children are met. But it is important to recognise that this is a shared responsibility and that this has implications for the role of the school management and collaboration with other professionals, other teachers and with parents. Staff development, therefore, is crucial and should provide all teachers and school management with an awareness of dyslexia.

Policy on dyslexia is also important and there are already some good examples of comprehensive policies on dyslexia at education authority and school level. Policies need to be comprehensive as they need to incorporate the training requirements, as well as the role of classroom teachers, in identification, assessment and curriculum planning in relation to identifying the barriers that can be faced by dyslexic children and how these barriers can be overcome.

The other key theme of the book is that of inclusion – this implies that the needs of all children with dyslexia should be met within mainstream school. It is, however, recognised in this book, particularly in Chapter 4, that inclusion can incorporate alternative networks of support that can cater for the needs of dyslexic children at certain points in their education.

It is important to recognise that while there are many trained dyslexia specialists and specialised dyslexia resources available, policies relating to the National Literacy Strategy and inclusion suggest that classroom teachers now have the key role to play in identification and planning for the learning of dyslexic children. Ideally this should be a shared responsibility but nevertheless this does place considerable onus on the class teacher to develop and present the curriculum in a dyslexia-friendly way.

This book discusses inclusion and curriculum planning and essentially aims to equip the class teacher with the knowledge and the confidence to deal with dyslexia within the curriculum, and in an inclusive educational setting.

Chapter 1

Understanding and Identifying Dyslexia

Dyslexia is a term that is frequently used in schools and in the wider community – yet a term that many would admit is surrounded by confusion and ambiguity. Such confusion does not help the teacher understand the needs of children with dyslexia and this can in fact give rise to some anxiety. It is the aim of this book to clarify the confusion surrounding dyslexia from the class teachers' perspective and to highlight some strategies for identification and teaching and particularly to provide a curriculum perspective in order to ensure that learners will have access to the full curriculum.

Definitions

One of the areas of confusion centres on issues relating to definitions of dyslexia. There is a range of definitions that are currently used to describe dyslexia. This can cause confusion particularly in relation to the identification of dyslexia, as the use of the label 'dyslexia' may depend on the specific identification criteria applied. Burden (2002) suggests that dyslexia is a 'convenience term' because it can embrace a number of different types of difficulties and, therefore, the term 'dyslexia' in itself is not helpful. While there is some validity in this – mainly because of the overlapping features between dyslexia and other types of difficulties – it is evading the issue to describe dyslexia as a convenience term.

There are some core characteristics of dyslexia that are important for identification and assessment and for the development of IEPs, teaching and curriculum materials. These characteristics – whatever the term used to describe them – can present considerable barriers to learning for children and young people in school. It may be helpful to view dyslexia from the perspective of attempting to identify and address the barriers to literacy and learning that can be experienced by the child. These barriers will be described throughout this book, but it is important to acknowledge that the means of addressing these barriers can lie within the classroom environment and curriculum differentiation as much as with the use of any specialised resources.

Confusion and consensus

The confusion that surrounds the use of the term 'dyslexia' has arisen for a number of reasons. As far back as 1978 the Warnock Report (DES, 1978) acknowledged the presence of children who had unexpected and unusual difficulties in literacy, but stated that the term 'dyslexia' was not helpful to describe these children and that the term 'specific learning difficulties' would be a more appropriate one to use. Education authorities, therefore, were reluctant to use the term 'dyslexia' and this was not helpful in the quest to clarify the term, nor to give teachers an understanding of dyslexia and to examine the implications of this for the classroom. The reluctance to use the term also gave rise to a vigorous (and largely successful) lobbying campaign by a range of pressure groups to have the term accepted and applied.

Policy and reports

An indication of how this situation has changed since the 1980s can be seen in recent government and education authority policy documents that have mentioned and, indeed in some cases, focused on policy, specifically for dyslexia. Both the Irish Republic (Task Report on Dyslexia 2001) and Northern Ireland Government (Task Group Report on Dyslexia 2002) have published extensive policy documents on dyslexia. Indeed, in the preface to the Northern Ireland task group report the Minister for Education indicated that the report highlighted a very real concern that provided challenges for all in education. This concern, he suggested, surrounds:

> particularly the need for training for classroom teachers in recognising where children have, or may have, dyslexia and in putting in place the means to address their difficulties.

Similarly, in England and Wales there have been vigorous dyslexia-friendly schools' campaigns that have been supported by the government in collaboration with the British Dyslexia Association. This has resulted in materials being widely circulated to schools and significant efforts to provide an education authority-wide attempt to identify and tackle dyslexia. Scotland has also witnessed collaboration between education authorities, the Scottish Executive, teacher education institutions and voluntary associations to develop teaching programmes, and resources for identification and intervention for dyslexia (Reid, 2001; Crombie, 2002).

Dyslexia research

As well as confusion stemming from the initial reluctance to use the term dyslexia, following the Warnock Report, the confusion has also occurred because the research field in dyslexia is a multi-faceted one, that can be characterised as much by disagreement as agreement. In short, there are research activities in different aspects of neurology brain structure, neurological processing, the cerebellum, visual cortex, as well as speech and language processing. Additionally, cognitive psychologists are involved in studies involving memory and dyslexia as well as the role of processing speed and the cognitive routes to literacy acquisition. This can present a confusing picture for teachers who are seeking straight-forward explanations of dyslexia and guidance for practice. The picture can be further confused by the range of alternative interventions (and often costly) programmes that have been developed for dyslexia (Reid, 2003). Silver (2001) comments that alternative programmes and controversial therapies develop too quickly, and the time from initial conception to acceptance of a particular idea is usually not long enough. This should take years and needs to be supported by research published in peer-reviewed journals. He suggests that there is too much anecdotal evidence that often convinces parents of the value of certain approaches, and it should be acknowledged that what works for one child may not be successful for another. The effect of research activities in neurological areas and the commercial thrust of alternative therapies have often resulted in teacher conferences on dyslexia being dominated by this type of information. It is crucial, therefore, that the focus for intervention should be firmly based in classroom practices.

Professional involvement and perspectives

The diversity in research in dyslexia has resulted in many professional and other groups being involved in suggestions for intervention. This can be confusing to both parents and teachers. For example, the following can each have some input into a case conference on a child with dyslexia:

- class teacher
- educational adviser for the education authority
- SENCO/ learning support
- educational psychologist
- clinical psychologist
- occupational therapist
- ICT specialist

- optometrist
- parents

The different research perspectives that can account for some of the confusion can be seen in the British Psychological Society (BPS) working party report into assessment of dyslexia (BPS, 1999). The report offers ten different hypotheses to explain and understand dyslexia. Some of these relate to cognitive aspects such as how children process information, some to reading characteristics such as phonological awareness and visual processing difficulties, and others to learning opportunities and environmental factors. This can provide some indication of the broad scope of dyslexia.

Hidden disability

There is now some agreement that dyslexia represents more than a reading difficulty.

While there are many well-enunciated principles for teaching children with dyslexia, a closer examination of these indicate that many of these principles incorporate good teaching practices which will in fact benefit all children.

Dyslexia can be described as a hidden disability because we may not know the person has dyslexia until they are put into a situation that requires skills in literacy or processing certain types of information. At school many children become skilled at covering up and compensating for their dyslexic difficulties, usually by avoiding reading aloud or writing as little as possible. Sometimes dyslexia can be misunderstood for laziness or lack of interest in school work. In reality that is far from the case – usually children with dyslexia extend more effort than others because of their difficulty, and may often become tired very easily as a result of this effort.

Programmes and resources

It is important therefore to ensure that class teachers have an understanding of dyslexia and of the strategies and supports that are appropriate and can be readily applied to the classroom without referring to costly commercially produced materials.

There is of course a wide range of programmes and resources which have been specifically developed for use for children with dyslexia, many of these are excellent and will be referred to in the following chapter of this book.

Characteristics of dyslexia

Hearing

The above diagram refers to the different aspects that are influential in an understanding of dyslexia. The ear represents the auditory aspects. These can be important in relation to developing phonological awareness. Phonological awareness is seen as being a crucial factor in dyslexia – that is, differentiating between sounds, especially sounds that are similar, remembering these sounds and identifying them in words. These aspects can present difficulties for dyslexic children.

Sight

The eye symbol in the above diagram represents the visual aspects of dyslexia. Some dyslexic children may have some visual disturbance when reading print and this can cause blurring, words merging and omissions of words or lines when reading. Coloured overlays for some children have been successful, as has the use of coloured background for text and the font characteristics and font size.

Connections

The symbol in the diagram above between the eye and the ear represents the neurological basis for dyslexia and the importance of neurological connections. These connections help with the integration of different skills such as visual/motor integration, as in copying, and auditory/kinaesthetic integration, as in listening and carrying out instructions. There is considerable research evidence that highlights the neurological basis of dyslexia and in particular the connecting pathways of the left and right hemispheres as well as aspects relating to the cerebellum and the magnocellular visual system. These factors affect processing speed as well as visual accuracy and co-ordination.

Motor skills

The symbol of the child on the bicycle represents the motor aspects of dyslexia. The cerebellum in particular has been implicated in this, and a number of dyslexic children will display fine motor and gross motor difficulties that can result in poor handwriting and/or clumsiness.

The core difficulties

The pencils and the book in the above diagram represent the core difficulties associated with dyslexia – reading, spelling and writing. These tasks are usually left hemisphere skills, apart from creative writing, which can be associated with the right hemisphere. The research indicates that dyslexic children have weaknesses in the left hemisphere so therefore tasks involving phonics, accuracy, sequencing and remembering will be more challenging and often more exhausting for the child with dyslexia.

Interaction

The last three symbols in the diagram above show a teacher with a student, the school building and a bowl of fruit. The teacher and the student highlight the importance of interaction. Quite often children with dyslexia need interaction with the teacher in order to provide the most appropriate cues, structure and to help develop connections with previous learning. This aspect cannot be emphasised strongly enough because if interaction does not take place, for example through teacher/pupil question and answer, then the dyslexic person may fail to grasp the underlying concepts and the information will be less meaningful. This interaction can lead to what is sometimes referred to as metacognition. This involves the student questioning him/herself as to why he/she thinks in a certain way. This type of self-questioning is an aspect of metacognition. This is dealt with in more detail in subsequent chapters of this book.

School ethos

The symbol of the school highlights the importance of the school ethos and the learning environment. It is important that the child feels comfortable in the school particularly since for many dyslexic children school represents a place of failure. It is crucial that this view is reversed and a welcoming and positive school environment can help greatly with this.

Diet

The bowl of fruit represents the role of diet in learning. Dyslexic children and indeed all children require a well-balanced diet to learn effectively. Research by Richardson (2002) highlights the importance of essential fatty acids to maximise efficient learning and that many children with dyslexia are deficient in Omega 3 and Omega 6 essential fatty acids.

The whole diagram seeks to highlight the breadth of the areas involved in dyslexia – it is not a narrow syndrome, but one that incorporates many aspects of language and of learning.

The role of the label

Usually the term 'dyslexia' is only applied after a fairly extensive assessment process as it is important that labels are not used unnecessarily. A label generally brings a set of expectations. These can relate to a more informed selection of resources, or a different set of expectations from parents, and perhaps teachers. While a label can be helpful, it can also be disadvantageous and may lead to a resignation that dyslexia can only be dealt with by 'experts'. This is a misguided assumption, and may lead the teacher to feel she/he possesses neither the skills, nor the training, to deal with dyslexia in the classroom. Yet there is, in fact, no specific approach that is universally recognised to deal with dyslexia. The notion of multi-sensory approaches involving the use of visual, auditory, kinaesthetic and tactile strategies are believed to be essential for children with dyslexia, yet such approaches are also useful for all children and indeed incorporate elements of good teaching. There are, however, many specific teaching programmes often used with children with dyslexia that are built around these approaches, as well as an enhanced understanding of the type of difficulties experienced by children with dyslexia.

The key point, therefore, in teaching children with dyslexia is knowledge of teaching, not access to resources. It is important that the teacher has knowledge and understanding of the type of difficulties associated with dyslexia and also of the actual child, i.e. his/her profile, background, difficulties, strengths and the strategies that have already been utilised. This is extremely important as the profile of strengths and difficulties presented by children with dyslexia can differ. This, therefore, means that the responsibility for teaching children with dyslexia lies, not with a 'specialist', but with class teachers who have the knowledge and the experience of adapting and differentiating teaching materials, and are able to adapt their teaching to suit the needs of the learner. Aspects relating to curriculum development are also crucial and the needs of children with dyslexia can be met, as much through careful planning of curriculum and teaching objectives, as through the use of specialised materials.

Dyslexia as a difference

Dyslexia can be described as a difference in the way some people process information. This means that reading accurately, and at speed, can be difficult for children with dyslexia, as can spelling accurately and writing in a structured manner. The individual with dyslexia can become confused when several instructions are given at the same time, and will usually have a poor short-term memory, difficulty with directional orientation, such as telling right from left and map reading. They may also have a word finding difficulty and in discussions and conversation may use inappropriate words – perhaps words that sound or look similar – such as 'were' and 'where' and 'there' and 'their'. They may also confuse syllables in words, or put these in the wrong order when writing or talking, such as 'preliminary' or 'elephant.' But essentially the characteristics can amount to a different way of processing information – they usually have a visual, right-brained global processing style and it is important to acknowledge the strengths in this style, as well as considering the difficulties.

Identification

When identifying dyslexia it is preferable to have both a rationale and a strategy for the assessment. Often a suspicion of the presence of dyslexic difficulties can be identified through observation, or through the results of routine assessments. This information, however, needs to be contextualised, so that an overall picture of the child's profile can be seen and evidence of dyslexia, if any, can be noted, and importantly the barriers to learning identified. This is necessary, as one of the purposes of identification of dyslexia is to identify the most appropriate teaching and learning approaches. Some general aspects relating to the purpose of an assessment include the following:

- identification of the learner's general strengths and weaknesses;
- indication of the learner's current level of performance in attainments;
- an explanation for the learner's lack of progress;
- identification of aspects of the learner's performance in reading, writing and spelling, which may typify a 'pattern of errors';
- identification of specific areas of competence;
- understanding of the student's learning style;
- indication of aspects of the curriculum that may interest and motivate the learner; and
- specific aspects of the curriculum that are challenging for the child.

Some of the specific characteristics that can be noted include the following:

Reading
- difficulty in recognising sounds in words;
- difficulty in remembering the combinations of letters that make up sounds such as 'ph' and 'th' and remembering these and using them in a word;
- sequencing the sounds and the letters in words in the correct order;
- substitution of words when reading aloud, for example saying 'car' for 'bus';
- difficulty with rhyming, remembering, for example nursery rhymes and remembering the sequence of the rhyme;
- may find it difficult to sound out sounds in words;
- reverses, omits or adds letters;
- loses the place when reading;
- may have difficulty with the sequence of the alphabet;
- difficulty pronouncing multi-syllabic words, even common ones;
- poor word attack skills – particularly with unknown words;
- reading speed tends to be slow and hesitant and often with little expression;
- reluctance to read for pleasure;
- reading comprehension tends to be better than single word reading; and
- confuses words which have the same or similar sounds – such as 'their' and 'there' and 'access' and 'assess'.

Spelling
- difficulty remembering spelling rules;
- making phonological errors in spelling, for example 'f' for 'ph';
- letters out of sequence;
- inconsistent use of some letters with similar sounds such as 's' and 'z';

9

- difficulty with word endings, for example using 'ie' for 'y';
- confusion or omission of vowels; and
- difficulty with words with double consonants such as 'commission'.

Writing
- inconsistent writing style;
- slow writing speed;
- inconsistent use of capital and small letters;
- reluctance to write any lengthy piece; and
- a sometimes unusual writing grip or sitting position.

Memory
- poor short-term memory which means probable difficulty remembering lists; and
- may also show signs of poor long-term memory which could be due to confusion at the time of learning or poor organisational strategies.

Organisation
- poor organisational strategies for learning; and
- poor organisation of timetable, materials, equipment and items needed for learning, such as remembering and organising homework notebook.

Movement
- may have difficulty with co-ordination and tasks such as tying shoelaces; and
- bumping into furniture in the classroom, tripping and frequently falling.

Speech development
- confusing similar sounds;
- poor articulation;
- difficulty blending sounds into words;
- poor awareness of rhyme;
- poor syntactic structure; and
- naming difficulties.

It is important to recognise that many of these factors above can be seen in a continuum of difficulties from mild to severe, and the extent and severity of these difficulties will have an impact on the assessment results and the subsequent recommendations for support.

Information processing

It can be suggested that dyslexia is an information processing difficulty. Information processing describes the interaction between the learner and the task. Essentially the information processing cycle has three main components. These are:

- **Input** – auditory, visual, tactile, kinaesthetic
- **Cognition** – memory, understanding, organising and making sense of information
- **Output** – reading aloud, talking, discussing, drawing, seeing, experiencing

Children with dyslexia can have difficulty at all three stages of this cycle. It is important, therefore, to draw on diagnostic data that involves these three stages. It can be useful to acknowledge this when identifying the difficulties experienced by the child. For example one can ask whether the same difficulties are experienced if the material is presented visually as opposed to auditorily. Perhaps the individual can learn more effectively if he/she is able to experience the actual learning through the kinaesthetic modality. Although this is related to teaching approaches it is crucial that this is acknowledged in the identification and assessment process as it is important that reasons for the difficulty are sought, and further, that a clear link can be forged between assessment and teaching approaches.

Assessment

Process and strategies
Dyslexia should not only be identified through the use of a test. Assessment for dyslexia is a process and that process involves much more than the administration of a test. The assessment needs to consider classroom and curriculum factors, as well as the specific difficulties and strengths shown by the child.

Specifically, assessment should consider three aspects – difficulties, discrepancies and differences, and these should relate to the classroom environment and the curriculum.

The central difficulty is usually related to the decoding, or the encoding, of print and this may be the result of different contributory factors. For example, some difficulties may include phonological processing, memory problems, organisational and sequencing difficulties, movement and co-ordination, language problems, or visual-perceptual/auditory-perceptual difficulties.

The discrepancies may be apparent in comparing decoding and reading/listening comprehension, between oral and written responses and in performances within the different subject areas of the curriculum.

It is also important to acknowledge the differences between individual children with dyslexia. The identification process should, therefore, also consider learning styles and cognitive styles. An appreciation of this can help to effectively link assessment and teaching.

Miscue analysis during oral reading

The strategy known as miscue analysis is based on the 'top-down' approach to reading that was developed from the work of Goodman (1976). Goodman argued that the reader first has to make predictions as to the most likely meaning of the text. Such predictions were based on how the reader perceived the graphic, syntactic and semantic information contained in the text.

Goodman suggested that by using miscue analysis a teacher can listen to a child read and determine whether a mistake or 'miscue' results. These miscues can arise from symbolic, syntactic or semantic errors. Symbolic errors would mean that the child has misread the actual letter(s) and this can be a result of a visual difficulty. Syntactic errors may occur when the child reads the word 'of' instead of 'for'. This would indicate that the child does not have the grammatical structures of sentences but can make a fairly good stab at the symbolic features of the word – even though it is still wrong. The other type of errors – semantic errors – are quite common in children with dyslexia as these kinds of errors would indicate the reader is relying heavily on context. An example of a semantic error would be reading the word 'bus' instead of 'car'.

An example of how miscue analysis can be used in a passage is shown on the following page.

Goodman used the phrase 'psycholinguistic guessing game' to describe how readers, especially poor readers, tackled print. This means that children used contextual and symbolic cues to read rather than decoding every word. If the child misread, this means they used the wrong cues, or failed to understand the meaning of the text and, therefore, could not use this to help them 'guess' the word.

This was a move away from the bottom-up model of reading that had, up until this point, dominated literacy teaching. The bottom-up model emphasises the decoding of individual letters and sounds by breaking words into phonemes – the sound component of words – and building up words and sentences from this. This implies the child needs to read accurately before any meaning can be extracted from the text. Goodman's view on the other hand suggested that even poor readers can extract meaning from text by using contextual and other cues. The essence of the top-down approach was that the reader started with the whole and moved to the 'parts'.

(The) Bad Dogs

On
Once there were two dogs. They lived in the *a* same village. One was called Spot. The other was called Lassie. They liked each other. They went/for runs on their own. One hot day they went for a long run. They ran and ran.
They came to a field. *Where* They sniffed new smells. They saw some white animals. *with* They were not dogs. They ran round *running* (and round) the animals. The animals made silly noises. The noises sounded like 'Baa-baa' *be-bu*. They were sheep.

Spot/said, 'We will *what* chase them out of the field.' They did so. The sheep were *with* frightened. Spot and/Lassie barked *barkened* loudly. They felt very clever/ *scared* They thought the sheep were silly. *with* *safe*
Then Lassie stood still. *stopped* Her ears went up. *hair* 'A man/is/coming. He has a big *Here* stick.' *stike*

Coding Symbols

MISCUE TYPE	ORIGINAL TEXT	ACTUAL RESPONSE	SYMBOL
Non-response (refusal)	The other was called Lassie.	The other was called _ _ _ _ _ _	Lassie
Substitution	Once there were two dogs	On there were two dogs	*On* Once there were two dogs
Omission	they ran round and round the animals	they ran round the animals	they ran round (and round)
Insertion	– to a field. They sniffed	– to a field where they sniffed	*Where* to a field. They sniffed
Reversal	They did so	so they did	They did so
Self-correction	Then Lassie stood still.	Then Lassie stopped-stood- still	Then Lassie *stopped* stood still
Hesitation	They went for runs	They went for -- runs	They went for /runs
Repetition	runs on their own	runs on their their own	runs on their own

(reproduced from Arnold, 1984, with permission from Hodder & Stoughton)

Goodman's theory gave impetus to the 'whole book approach' and in fact fuelled what is known as the 'literacy wars'. This term describes the controversy over top-down approaches (meaning and language experiences) and bottom-up (decoding and phoneme) approaches to teaching reading. The important point for our purposes here is that Goodman's approaches also gave impetus to a more diagnostic approach to the assessment of reading. This approach was further emphasised by Marie Clay with the Reading Recovery Programme (Clay, 1979) which also used miscue analysis as one of the fundamental approaches to diagnosing a child's reading level.

One of the important aspects about miscue analysis is that it can help the teacher make deductions about the reader's understanding of the text. For example, if the child read 'the poor horse bolted his food' instead of 'the scared horse bolted fast' this would indicate that he/she has little real understanding of the text apart from the fact it concerns a horse. This would likely indicate a difficulty with the semantics of the text, since the guess does not properly fit the context. The syntactic flow of the sentence appears to be correct and there is some attempt to represent the symbols.

Miscues, therefore, can inform the teacher about how the reader perceives the text and the pattern of errors that may exist. It is also important to observe whether the miscue is self-corrected, the graphic or phonemic similarity between the expected response and the observed response (what the child actually says) and whether the miscue produces syntactically or semantically acceptable text.

It is, therefore, possible to obtain useful data on the child's reading pattern by observing the reading errors and noting the significance of these oral errors.

The type of errors often noted in miscue analysis and the significance of these are shown below:

Omissions
These may occur if the child is reading for meaning rather than the actual print. He/she may omit small words that do not add anything significant to the meaning of the passage.

Additions
These may reflect superficial reading with perhaps an over-dependence on context clues.

Substitutions
These can be visual or semantic substitutions and they may reflect an over-dependence on context clues.

Repetitions

These may indicate poor directional attack, especially if the child reads the same line again. These may also indicate some hesitancy on the part of the child perhaps being unable to read the next word in the line.

Reversals

These may reflect the lack of left–right orientation. Reversals may also indicate some visual difficulty and perhaps a lack of reading for meaning.

Hesitations

These can occur when the reader is unsure of the text and perhaps lacking in confidence in reading. For the same reason that repetitions may occur, the reader may also be anticipating a difficult word later in the sentence.

Self-corrections

These would occur when the reader becomes more aware of meaning and less dependent on simple word recognition. It is important to recognise the extent of self-corrections as this can indicate that the child does have an understanding of the passage. Children with dyslexia can show most of the miscues noted above, especially as often they read for meaning and, therefore, additions and substitutions can be quite common.

Phonological assessment

To a great extent this can be carried out by the teacher from teacher-adapted materials or indeed through observation of the child's reading pattern. Gorrie and Parkinson (1995) have provided a structured set of phonological assessment procedures and an example of the score sheet showing the types of aspects assessed is shown on the following page.

The procedures developed by Gorrie and Parkinson consist of an assessment and a linked programme. The programme contains three components – assessment, games and resources. The assessment section, as can be noted above, provides a very detailed analysis of the child's phonological awareness and covers the following areas:

- polysyllabic word/non word repetition and recognition;
- syllable segmentation, deletion of prefixes and suffixes and deletion of syllables;
- intra-syllable segmentation such as detection of onset and rime at rhyme judgement and production; and
- phoneme segmentation such as blending, detection and deletion of initial and final phonemes.

15

Phonological awareness procedure – score sheet

Name _____ Date _____ CA _____

Assessment	Page	Raw score	%	Comment
Polysyllabic Word/Non-word 1.1 Repetition – Word – Non-word 1.2 Recognition				
Syllable Segmentation 2.1 Detection of Syllables 2.2 Counting Syllables 2.3 Production of Syllables 2.4 Compound Word 2.5 Deletion of Prefixes & Suffixes 2.6 Deletion of Syllables				
Intra-Syllable Segmentation 3.1 Detection of Onset 3.2 Detection of Rime 3.3 Deletion of Onset 3.4 Production of Onset 3.5 Judgement of Rhyme 3.6 Production of Rhyme				
Phoneme Segmentation 4.1 Blending 4.2 Detection (clapping) 4.3 Detection (saying sounds) 4.4 Deletion of Initial Phonemes 4.5 Deletion of Final Phonemes				
Recommendations				

(reproduced from Gorrie and Parkinson, 1995, with permission from Stass Publications)

These aspects can be readily observed by the teacher and an appropriate programme developed from these observations. This of course will mean focusing on the bottom-up aspects of reading. Yet whatever view or perspective one adopts in relation to models of reading, it is crucial and fairly widely accepted that all children need a basic grasp of literacy structures before they can benefit from contextual top-down reading strategies.

There are also standardised phonological assessments available and recommended for use in an assessment for dyslexia. One such assessment is detailed below:

The Phonological Assessment Battery (PhAB)
The battery consists of five measures:

- Alliteration test
- Rhyme test
- Naming speed test
- Fluency test
- Spoonerism test

This test may to be very suitable to use to assess dyslexic difficulties. There is good evidence that dyslexic children have difficulty with rhyme and alliteration and some researchers have indicated that naming speed is in itself a significant feature of dyslexic difficulties (Wolf and O'Brien, 2000; Nicolson and Fawcett, 2001).

The Phonological Assessment Battery (Frederickson et al 1997) can be accessed by all teachers and is available from NFER-Nelson, www.nfer-nelson.co.uk.

Screening/baseline assessment
There are some issues that can be raised in relation to screening and baseline assessment. These include:

- What is the most desirable age (or ages) for children to be screened?
- Which skills, abilities and attainments in performances should children be screened for?
- How should the results of any screening procedures be used?

It is important that the results of screening and baseline assessments are used diagnostically and not to prematurely label children. There are some screening tests that have been developed specifically to identify the possibility of dyslexia. These can yield very useful information but should be used in conjunction with other data obtained from observations made by the teacher of the child's work and progress in class, and in different areas of the curriculum. These include the following:

Bangor Dyslexia Test (LDA, Cambridge, www.LDAlearning.com)
This is a commercially available short screening test developed from
work conducted at Bangor University (Miles, 1983). The test is divided
into the following sections:

- left–right (body parts);
- repeating polysyllabic words;
- subtraction;
- tables;
- months forward/reversed;
- digits forward/reversed;
- b–d confusion;
- familial incidence.

It is important to note that this test is only intended as a screening
device to find out whether the subject's difficulties are, or are not,
typically dyslexic and may offer a contribution towards an understanding of the subject's difficulties. It should not, therefore, be seen as a
definitive diagnosis.

Dyslexia Screening Test (DST)
The authors of this test (Fawcett and Nicolson, 1996) indicate that it
was developed due to both the wider theoretical understanding of
dyslexia, particularly since the publication of the earlier Bangor Dyslexia
Test, and the changes in the British educational system, particularly
relating to the formal procedures for assessing whether children have
special educational needs. It may also have a use, according to the
authors, of assessing whether some children should have concessionary
extra time in examinations.

The screening instrument can be used for children between 6.6 to
16.5 years of age, although there is also an alternative version developed
by the same authors for younger children, Dyslexia Early Screening Test
(Nicolson and Fawcett, 1996). The test consists of the following
attainment tests:

- one minute reading;
- two minute spelling;
- one minute writing.

and the following diagnostic tests:

- rapid naming;
- bead threading;
- postural stability;

- phonemic segmentation;
- backwards digit span;
- nonsense passage reading;
- verbal and semantic fluency.

These tests are consistent with the current theoretical standing of dyslexia, particularly in relation to the research on phonological difficulties and speed of processing. As in all screening tests there is some limit on the value of the information but the wide range of factors considered in this test does enhance its value as a screening device.

The Dyslexia Screening tests can be accessed by all teachers and are available from the Psychological Corporation, 24–28 Oval Road, London, NW1 7DX, e-mail: cservice@harcourtbrace.com.

Cognitive Profiling System (CoPS) (Lucid Creative Ltd, Beverley, Yorkshire, UK)
This is a computerised screening programme and constitutes a user-friendly package, complete with facilities for student registration, graphic report and print out of results. CoPS is used in over 3,500 primary schools in the UK and elsewhere in the world (Singleton 2002). There is also the CoPS baseline assessment (Singleton, Thomas and Horne, 1998).

In 1999 Lucid also published LASS – Lucid Assessment System for Schools – Secondary (Horne, Singleton and Thomas, 1999) and in 2001 this was followed up by LASS Junior for primary schools. These programmes are now used in over 1,000 primary and secondary schools in the UK.

Listening and Literacy Index (Weedon and Reid, 2001) available from Hodder and Stoughton (see later in this chapter)

Quest-Screening, Diagnostic and Support Kit (Second Edition, 1995) NFER-Nelson – www.nfer-nelson.co.uk
Quest consists of group screening tests and individual diagnostic tests. The responses from the diagnostic test together with the associated workbooks can help in the planning of learning support programmes for pupils with difficulties in language and mathematics

The screening is related to Key Stage 1 of the National Curriculum in England and Wales and Key Stage 1 of Standards of Attainment in the National Curriculum in Northern Ireland as well as Level A of the 5–14 curriculum in Scotland.

Essentially, the materials aim to identify pupils at the beginning of the third year of schooling who may require support in learning. The materials, reading and number screening tests and reading and number diagnostic tests are accompanied by a series of workbooks, reading quest, looking quest, writing quest and number quest and a teacher's quest manual.

These materials represent a comprehensive list that can identify children's difficulties early and offer a good example of materials that effectively link assessment and teaching. Examples of the test descriptions in the Quest Diagnostic Reading Test are shown below:

- pre-reading;
- auditory discrimination;
- auditory sequential memory;
- visual discrimination;
- visual sequencing;
- visuo-motor co-ordination.

Word search skills
- sight vocabulary;
- letter recognition (sounds);
- simple blends;
- beginnings and endings;
- digraphs, silent 'e' rule and silent letters;
- word building;
- reading comprehension.

Special Needs Assessment Profile (Weedon and Reid, 2003) Hodder Murray, www.hoddertests.co.uk and also at www.SNAPassessment.com The Special Needs Assessment Profile (SNAP) is a computer-aided diagnostic assessment and profiling package that makes it possible to 'map' each students' own mix of problems on to an overall matrix of learning, behavioural and other difficulties. From this, clusters and patterns of weaknesses and strengths help to identify the core features of a student's difficulties – visual, dyslexic, dyspraxic, phonological, attentional or any other of the 15 key deficits targeted – and suggests a diagnosis that points the way forward for that individual student. It provides a structured profile which yields an overview at the early stages of 'School Action' in the Code of Practice and also informs the process of external referral at 'School Action Plus'.

SNAP involves four steps:
- *Step 1 (Pupil Assessment Pack):* structured questionnaire checklists for completion by class teachers and parents give an initial 'outline map' of the child's difficulties.
- *Step 2 (CD-ROM):* the SENCO or Learning Support staff chart the child's difficulties, using the CD-ROM to identify patterns and target any further diagnostic follow-up assessments to be carried out at Step 3.

- *Step 3 (User's Kit):* focused assessments from a photocopiable resource bank of quick diagnostic 'probes' yield a detailed and textured understanding of the child's difficulties.
- *Step 4 (CD-ROM):* the computer-generated profile yields specific guidance on support (including personalised information sheets for parents) and practical follow-up.

The kit helps to facilitate the collaboration between different groups of professionals and between professionals and parents which is extremely vital in order to obtain a full picture of the students' abilities and difficulties. There is a dedicated website that can be accessed by anyone that contains a number of ideas on teaching to cover difficulties associated with 15 different specific learning difficulties. The website is www.SNAPassessment.com.

Checklists

There are many variations of checklists for identifying dyslexia. This in itself highlights the need to treat checklists with considerable caution. Checklists are not, in any form, a definitive diagnosis of dyslexia and are, therefore, of fairly limited value, except perhaps for a preliminary screening to justify a more detailed assessment. Some checklists can, however, provide a range of information that may produce a picture of the child's strengths and weaknesses, such as the one shown below. Even these, however, are still very limited and no substitution for a comprehensive and contextual assessment.

Checklist on reading
- sight vocabulary;
- sound blending;
- use of contextual clues;
- attempting unknown vocabulary;
- eye tracking;
- difficulty keeping the place;
- speech development;
- motivation in relation to reading material;
- word naming difficulty;
- omits words;
- omits phrases;
- omits whole lines.

Checklist for written work

- directional difficulty;
- difficulty in associating visual symbol with verbal sound;
- liability to sub-vocalise sounds prior to writing;
- unusual spelling pattern;
- handwriting difficulty;
- difficulty with cursive writing;
- uses capitals and lower case interchangably and inconsistently;
- poor organisation of work on page.

This form of assessment can provide some general data on the broad areas of difficulty experienced by the child. For example, the teacher may decide the child has a pronounced difficulty in the use of contextual cues, but this does not provide information as to why this difficulty persists and the kind of difficulties the pupil experiences with contextual cues. Does the child use contextual cues on some occasions and under certain conditions? Clearly this type of assessment, though useful, is limited and the teacher would be required to carry out further investigations to obtain a further picture of the difficulty.

Discrepancies

An approach to assessment that can be readily carried out by the teacher can involve the noting of discrepancies between different components of reading. These can include the following:

- decoding test (non-words reading test);
- word reading test;
- phonological awareness test;
- listening comprehension test;
- reading comprehension test.

The information gleaned from this type of assessment strategy can be compared and any obvious discrepancies can be noted. For example, a child with dyslexia may have a low score on a decoding test, and particularly one that involves non-words, while in the listening comprehension test he/she may score considerably higher. This strategy was one of the motivating factors for the development of the Listening and Literacy Index (Weedon and Reid, 2001) which is described below.

Listening and Literacy Index (Weedon and Reid, 2001) Hodder Murray, www.hoddertests.co.uk
The Listening and Literacy Index (Weedon and Reid, 2001) comprises group tests for profiling literacy development and identifying specific

learning difficulties. It contains linked standardised tests of listening, reading and spelling and is designed for use by the classroom teacher with whole-class groups. The tests have been standardised with a large UK sample and the handbook contains norms, guidelines for scoring and teaching follow-up. There are four sub-tests:

- *listening* – which assesses the child's ability to understand spoken language about everyday situations;
- *regular spelling* – which assesses phonological processing and memory;
- *sight word spelling* – which assesses visual processing and memory; and
- *reading comprehension* – which assesses the ability to read silently, for meaning.

The results of this test can display comparisons between these factors and this may provide an early indicator of the presence, or at least the risk, of dyslexia or any other specific learning difficulty. For example in the comparison between listening and the other scores it may be noted that a child who can listen well and with understanding, but whose spelling is poor and whose silent reading is laborious, may have a specific difficulty of a dyslexic type. If sight word spelling is better than regular spelling there may be an auditory difficulty. Where the two tasks that need sustained attention (listening and reading comprehension) are relatively weak, there may be an attention difficulty.

Differences

Learning context

When identifying and assessing the nature and degree of the difficulty experienced by the child, it is important to take into account the learning context. This context, depending on the learner's preferred style, can either exacerbate the difficulty or minimise the problem. The contextual factors below should, therefore, be considered:

- classroom environment;
- teaching style;
- the nature of the task;
- materials/resources.

Wearmouth and Reid (2002) suggest that in order to plan appropriate teaching approaches for children with dyslexia and other special needs there has been a move away from the solely 'medical' model of difficulties in learning to one that recognises the interactive nature of difficulties in learning. This envisages a broader concept of the nature of 'special needs' and how these can be identified and addressed.

This is essentially an 'interactive model', and the focus is on the barriers to pupils' learning that may arise as a result of the interaction between the characteristics of the student and what is offered through teaching and the available resources. So while cognitive assessment of pupils who may have dyslexia is important, it is also crucial to include interactive aspects in the assessment criteria. Therefore, it is important to assess the learning environment in which pupils acquire literacy. Difficulties in literacy development can be seen as a function of the interaction between within-child and environmental factors. It therefore follows that there must be an assessment of both the student's characteristics and also of the learning environment.

Environmental factors can be examined by observing how the child performs in different settings with different types of support. The use of a framework for collecting this type of data can yield considerable information and can complement the results from more formal assessment. Such observational assessment can be diagnostic because it is flexible, adaptable and can be used in natural settings with interactive activities. Reid and Given (2000) have developed such a framework – the Interactive Observational Style Identification (IOSI).

A summary of this is shown below:

Emotional motivation
- What topics, tasks and activities interest the child?
- What kind of prompting and cueing is necessary to increase motivation?
- What kind of incentives motivate the child – leadership opportunities, working with others, free time or physical activity?

Persistence
- Does the child stick to a task without breaks until completion?
- Are frequent breaks necessary when working on difficult tasks?

Responsibility
- To what extent does the child take responsibility for his/her own learning?
- Does the child attribute success or failure to self or others?

Structure
- Are the child's personal effects (desk, clothing, materials, well organised or cluttered?
- How does the child respond to someone imposing organisational structure on him/her?

Social interaction
- When is the child's best work accomplished – when working alone, with another, or in a small group?
- Does the child ask for approval or need to have work checked frequently?

Communication
- Does the child give the main events and gloss over the details?
- Does the child interrupt others when they are talking?

Cognitive modality preference
- What type of instructions does the child most easily understand – written, oral or visual?
- Does the child respond more quickly and easily to questions about stories heard or read?
- Is the child's learning sequential or simultaneous?
- Does the child begin with one step and proceed in an orderly fashion or have difficulty following sequential information?
- Is there a logical sequence to the child's explanations or do her/his thoughts bounce around from one idea to another?
- Impulsive / reflective
- Are the child's responses rapid and spontaneous or delayed and reflective?
- Does the child seem to consider past events before taking action?

Physical mobility
- Does the child move around the class frequently or fidget when seated?
- Does the child like to stand or walk while learning something new?

Food intake
- Does the child snack, or chew on a pencil when studying?

Time of day
- During which time of day is the child most alert?
- Is there a noticeable difference between morning work completed and afternoon work?

Reflection sound
- Does the child seek out places that are particularly quiet?

Light
- Does the child like to work in dimly lit areas or say that the light is too bright?

Temperature
- Does the child leave his/her coat on when others seem warm?

Furniture design
- When given a choice does the child sit on the floor, lie down, or sit in a straight chair to read?

Metacognition
- Is the child aware of his/her learning style strengths?
- Does the child demonstrate internal assessment of self by asking questions such as:
- Have I done this before?
- How did I tackle it?
- What did I find easy?
- Why did I find it easy or difficult?
- What did I learn?
- What do I have to do to accomplish this task?
- How should I tackle it?
- Should I tackle it the same way as before?

Prediction
- Does the child make plans and work towards goals or let things happen?

Feedback
- How does the child respond to different types of feedback?
- How much external prompting is needed before the child can access previous knowledge?

There are many manifestations of learning style and the learning environment. One method however that can be used to begin the observation process is to select one of the learning aspects and progress from there. The insights usually become greater as observation progresses. Information on learning styles can also be obtained by asking the student questions about their own preferences for learning. This can be achieved with very young children as well as secondary aged students. Students are usually aware of their own preferences, for example if they prefer to learn with background music or if they prefer silence when studying.

Formative and summative assessment

Individual education plans or individual profiles have become important tools in planning programmes of study for individual students who experience difficulty in literacy. In drawing up these individual programmes the assessment of students can be both formative and summative. It is important, therefore, not to view assessment as a one-off final diagnosis of a difficulty, but it should be primarily formative and help to form a programme, monitor progress, as well as provide pointers in relation to the child's strengths and weaknesses.

Dynamic assessment

Whilst standardised assessment can provide information on the student's level of attainments in comparison with peers, it is static since it emphasises what the learner can do unaided, but does not provide information about the learner's thinking processes. This is important for children who may have dyslexia as it is suggested that children with dyslexia may have good thinking skills but be unable to fully access these skills due to difficulties in either understanding the question, or in accessing the necessary print materials to express the answer in written form. 'Dynamic assessment' is the term used to describe the assessment that focuses on the process of learning. The strategies being used by the learner are identified and can also be a useful teaching tool through the development of concepts and ideas during teacher/student interaction. An example of this is reciprocal teaching, which consists of a dialogue between teacher and student for the purpose of jointly constructing the meaning of text and, therefore, can combine assessment and teaching.

Information from text

Assessment instruments are often based on restrictive criteria, examining what the student may be expected to know, often at a textual level. However, they may ignore other rich sources of information that can inform about the student's thinking, both cognitive and affective, and information that can provide suggestions for teaching. Ulmer and Timothy (1999) developed an alternative assessment framework based on 'retelling' as an instructional and assessment tool. This indicated that informative assessment of a student's comprehension could take place by using criteria relating to how the student retells a story. Ulmer and Timothy suggested the following criteria:

- *textual* – what the student remembered;
- *cognitive* – how the student processed the information; and
- *affective* – how the student felt about the text.

Their two-year study indicated that, of the teachers in the study assessed for textual information, only 31 per cent looked for cognitive indicators and 25 per cent for affective. Yet the teachers who did go beyond the textual found rich information. Some examples of information provided by the teachers indicated that by assessing beyond the textual level in relation to the use of the retelling method of assessment could provide evidence of the student's 'creative side' and they discovered that students could go 'beyond the expectations when given the opportunity'. This is a good example of how looking for alternative means of assessing can link with the student's understandings of the text.

Wray (1994) provides a description of some of the skills shown by good readers which can provide a good example of metacognitive awareness in reading. Good readers, according to Wray, usually:

- generate questions while they read;
- monitor and resolve comprehension problems;
- utilise mental images as they read;
- re-read when necessary; and
- self-correct if an error has been made when reading.

These factors can help to ensure that the reader has a clear picture of the purpose of reading and an understanding of the text about to be read. There is considerable evidence to suggest that pre-reading discussion can enhance reading fluency and understanding.

Summary

This chapter has suggested that the term 'dyslexia' should be used, but only after an extended assessment process. This process will involve observation, information from the classroom situation, from the curriculum and from parents, as well as data from any standardised assessments used. The class teacher, however, has a key role to play in this. It is important that teachers identify children at risk of dyslexia and attempt to deal with this at as early a stage as possible. There are in fact some screening instruments, such as the Dyslexia Early Screening Test, the Pre-School Screening Test (Fawcett, Nicolson and Lee, 2001) and the Listening and Literacy Index (Weedon and Reid, 2001), as well as computer screening tests (Singleton, 2002), that can identify children at an early stage who are at risk of dyslexia and literacy failure. Yet, even without reference to these early screening tests, it is possible for the class teacher, by using some observational strategies looking at phonological awareness and the error behaviour of the child in literacy, to note if any of the characteristics of dyslexia mentioned in this chapter are present.

It is also crucial that assessment information should not be only confined to identifying difficulties in literacy, as dyslexia can have wider implications than that. The learning process can be revealing and this can have implications for how the child with dyslexia functions in the classroom. It is also important, therefore, to acknowledge more general factors as well as metacognitive factors associated with learning. Not only will these yield important information for the assessment, but will also help to link assessment with teaching and this will guide the teacher in the development of appropriate curriculum and teaching materials. This will be the main focus for the remainder of this book.

Chapter 2

Teaching Approaches and Learning Strategies

Teaching and learning are deliberately linked together in this chapter. These two factors highlight the interactive nature of dealing with dyslexia in the classroom, and particularly the need to engage with the learner to foster higher order thinking skills, as well as those relating more directly to the acquisition of literacy. The actual process of learning is an important consideration. This involves helping the learner to engage with the topic in order to develop understanding and to connect the new information to their background knowledge of the subject. This can be done through the learner asking the most appropriate questions to develop this understanding. Many learners, including children with dyslexia, may have difficulty asking the right questions and need to rely on a structure and prompts provided by the teacher. This interaction helps the learner make connections between their existing knowledge and the new information to be learnt. Making such connections is an important element in learning, and it is often this – making connections – that can be challenging for learners with dyslexia.

Often the learning route selected by children with dyslexia is not a straightforward one. If teachers ask dyslexic learners how they achieved a response they may be surprised at the reply. Very often problem-solving activities for students with dyslexia can involve many steps to obtain an end result – perhaps to some this may seem wasteful of effort and perhaps a cumbersome method of obtaining a response. This type of problem-solving process engaged in by the dyslexic learner can be described as the 'right brain route' as opposed to the 'left brain route'. The following figure highlights the skills usually associated with each of these hemispheres. The 'right brain route' may be seen as a different way of gathering information, but can actually lead to creative ideas. Essentially it means that there may be a tendency for divergent thinking and processing laterally rather than in a linear fashion. It is important to encourage the dyslexic learner to adopt his/her own style of processing information and supporting them along the way. Sometimes, however, in subjects such as mathematics taking too many steps to get the right response may lead to mistakes and for that reason it is important that the student can explain to the teacher how he/she obtained a response.

Skills that can be associated with the hemispheres:

Left hemisphere	**Right hemisphere**
• handwriting	• spatial awareness
• language	• shapes and patterns
• reading	• mathematical computation
• phonics	• colour sensitivity
• locating details and facts	• singing and music
• talking and reciting	• art expression
• following directions	• creativity
• listening	• visualisation
• auditory association	• feelings and emotions

One of the key points to emerge from acknowledging the different routes to learning is the role of the learning experience. This, in itself, is an important factor, particularly for the learner with dyslexia and it is crucial that dyslexic learners actively engage in the learning process as far as possible using their own learning preferences. This may result in a more indirect route to solving a problem and as a result can take more time than expected. Additional time, therefore, should be allocated for this purpose. Often this type of right hemisphere learning process can be an enjoyable experience for a learner with dyslexia, and can result in additional knowledge and skills being accessed, quite apart from those intended in the actual task. Usually right brain approaches to learning can promote creativity and this is a factor that should not be overlooked.

Processes of learning

Learning is a cognitive process and this is important for children with dyslexia as often the difficulties they experience are of a cognitive nature.

Cognition refers to thinking and the different processes the learner engages in during thinking, problem-solving and learning. These processes include short and long-term memory, processing speed and processing style as well as the use of background information and previous knowledge.

How information is processed and how the curriculum, learning and teaching materials are presented are important considerations in learning. Dealing with dyslexia in the classroom, however, is not only about an acknowledgement and recognition of the child's difficulties, but must also incorporate factors such as curriculum development and the classroom environment. A holistic perspective needs to be adopted and not merely the factors relating to the cognitive difficulties experienced by the child. The factors that are important for successful learning therefore include:

- information processing;
- curriculum development;
- learning styles;
- strategies for learning;
- teaching style; and
- the classroom and school context.

Information processing

The stages of the information-processing cycle can relate to input, cognition and output.

Students with dyslexia, as indicated in the previous chapter, may experience difficulties at any, or each, of these stages. Some suggestions for practical strategies for dealing with each of these stages can include:

Input

At the input stage it is important to:

- present information in small units;
- monitor at frequent intervals to ensure that the student is comprehending;
- utilise overlearning, and vary this, using a range of materials and strategies; and
- present key points at the initial stage of learning new material.

Cognition

At the cognition stage it can be important to:

- encourage organisational strategies to help with learning;
- organise new material to be learned into meaningful chunks or categories;
- relate the new information to previous knowledge to ensure that concepts are clearly understood;
- place the information into a meaningful framework;
- utilise specific memory strategies, such as mind mapping and mnemonics; and
- monitor and assess the new learning frequently.

Output

At the output stage:

- use headings and subheadings in written work to help provide a structure;
- encourage the use of summaries in order to identify the key points; and
- assess learning at each point.

The points above are general points and these will be developed throughout this chapter. It is worth recognising at this point, however, that the effects of dyslexia can be minimised for the learner if the teaching, assessment, presentation and development of the curriculum acknowledges these potential cognitive difficulties.

Teaching – principles

Multi-sensory

There are a considerable number of intervention strategies for teaching reading and spelling to children with dyslexia. Many of these incorporate elements of what can be described as good teaching and are normally of a multi-sensory nature. That is they incorporate visual, auditory, kinaesthetic and tactile elements. This is important as dyslexic children often have difficulty receiving information using the auditory modality and it is crucial to ensure that they receive teaching input through their stronger modalities – these are usually the visual and kinaesthetic modalities. Kinaesthetic activities in particular are important as these imply that the learner is experiencing learning – this can be through drama, poetry or field trips and excursions, but it is important that the 'experience' is evident and the learner needs to be active and participatory throughout this experience.

Overlearning

Dyslexic children also require considerable overlearning. This does not mean pure repetition of teaching through repetitive rehearsal, but rather the use of a range of teaching approaches to ensure that the same words or skills are being taught in different situations. If a new word is learnt in, for example the class reader, it is important that this word is used in other contexts and the connections are deliberately made, and made clear to the learner. This also applies to spelling rules and many spelling patterns can lend themselves quite easily to overlearning through the use of the pattern in different words.

Automaticity

One of the reasons why overlearning is an important element in teaching dyslexic children is that they often take longer than some other children to achieve automaticity. This term refers to the consolidation of skills that learners normally achieve through practice. It is suggested that children with dyslexia take a longer period of time and require more varied input than some other children to acquire automaticity. This can become clear when after a period of teaching a particular word or skill, the learner may still not have mastery in these skills. This can be particularly the case if there is a break such as a holiday or even the weekend, when the word and the skills associated with the word have not been used. This is one of the reasons why dyslexic children need a considerable amount of practice in reading, both material that is below their level and above. Reading material below their level will ensure some practice in reading and help with automaticity and reading material above their level will help to provide the development of comprehension and strategies associated with context and comprehension as well as the use of inferential strategies. This can help the dyslexic person become more efficient at predicting and using inferences – these skills are necessary for comprehension especially if the reader has a low level of decoding skills.

Structure

It is important that all learning experiences should be structured to meet the needs of children with dyslexia within the classroom situation. Crombie (2002) suggests that structuring learning requires more than knowing the teaching order of the points that children must learn. The aspects and techniques that apply to the teaching process that will make the learning experiences worthwhile must also be considered. Crombie suggests that children who are being taught to spell will need to 'tune in' to words and sounds. If they do not, and are not aware of the sounds they are hearing, then spelling will be affected. For example, if a child is required to spell a word, but is unaware of the order of the sounds being heard, jumbling of letters is likely to occur, unless visual memory can compensate for this weakness. Training the child to repeat words to him/herself, while listening to the order of the sounds, is therefore time well spent.

The important point about this is that such skills may not be learnt automatically by children with dyslexia and often these need to be explicitly taught. As indicated above, this teaching needs to be multi-sensory and needs to actively engage the learner in the learning process. There are many examples of how this can be achieved and there are many game-type activities, that are discussed below, that can help with this.

Practice

There is also a strong view that phonically-based programmes are the most appropriate for dyslexic children. This, however, needs to be considered in the light of the individual child's learning and literacy needs and these may vary for different children.

Game-type activities can be extremely helpful in both engaging the learner and also ensuring that the necessary phonically based element is included. Some examples of these are the interactive literacy games from Crossbow Education, 41 Sawpit Lane, Brocton, Stafford, ST17 0TE, www.crossboweducation.com.

Crossbow Education specialise in games for children with dyslexia and produce activities on literacy, numeracy and study skills. These include Spingoes, and Onset and Rime Spinner Bingo, which comprises a total of 120 games using onset and rime; Funics, a practical handbook of activities to help children to recognise and use rhyming words, blend and segment syllables, identify initial phonemes and link sounds to symbols. Funics is produced by Maggie Ford and Anne Tottman and available from Crossbow Education. Crossbow also produce literacy games including Alphabet Lotto, which focuses on early phonics, Bing-Bang-Bong and CVC Spring, which help develop competence in short vowel sounds and Deebees which is a stick and circle board game to deal with b/d confusion.

They also have a board game called Magic-E Spinit and Hotwords – a five-board set for teaching and reinforcing 'h' sounds such as 'wh', 'sh', 'ch', 'th', 'ph', 'gh' and silent 'h'; Oh No, a times table photocopiable game book; Tens 'n' Units, which consists of spinning board games which help children of all ages practice the basics of place value in addition and subtraction.

Games and practical activities are also available from Multi-Sensory Learning, Highgate House, Grooms' Lane, Creaton, Northants, NN6 8NN; Tel: 01604 505000; www.msl-online.net; www.curriculumonline.gov.uk. The games include homophone games designed to improve spelling and recognition of 120 key words. The pack includes lotto scorers and coloured counters; a vowel discrimination game which helps to increase auditory awareness and improve word-attack skills; domino word chunks and a dyslexia games manual which has 50 pages of games and activities suitable for all ages in photocopiable format. The manual includes word games, memory games, sequencing activities, mnemonics, free writing suggestions and rhyme songs.

Such games and activities described above should be multi-sensory and the learner would normally be actively engaged in the task. This type of active and kinaesthetic engagement is ideal for children with dyslexia.

Programmes and strategies

Reid (2003) discusses many of the programmes that can be used for children with dyslexia but it is important to note here that those that are specialised are not necessarily the most appropriate in the classroom situation. Many of the individualised approaches (see below) are essentially one-to-one approaches and often require some specialised training. For that reason the support approaches, and those described as assisted learning and whole-school approaches, can be more appropriate for the classroom teacher.

Many of the support approaches can be improvised by the classroom teacher.

The range of approaches to support children with dyslexia includes the following:

Individualised approaches
Alphabetic Phonics
Alpha to Omega
Bangor Dyslexia Teaching System
Hickey Language Course
*Letterland
Orton-Gillingham Method
Reading Recovery Programme
*Spelling Made Easy
Slingerland
Sound Linkage
Skill Teach
Toe by Toe
THRASS
Units of Sound

Assisted learning programmes
Apprenticeship Approach
Paired Reading
Peer Tutoring
Reciprocal Teaching
Cued Spelling

Support approaches and strategies
Aston Portfolio
Simultaneous Oral Spelling
Counselling Approaches
**Phonic Codecracker/ Crackerspell
Specialised Software Programs
Neuro-Motor Programmes
Special Needs Manual – Reason and Boote
Study Skills
Quest Materials
Visual Acuity Activities
Word Games
Computer Programs
Davis Re-orientation Programme
Multi-sensory Teaching System for Reading (MTSR)
Educational Kinesiology
DDAT

Whole-school approaches
Counselling Strategies
Literacy Projects
Study Skills Programmes
Thinking Skills
Consultancy

These can also be used as the main teaching programme for the whole class.
**This can also be used as an individualised programme.*
(from Reid, 2003)

Language experience

Although many of the recognised approaches for dyslexic children are phonically based, it is also important that top-down approaches to reading are considered. These will help dyslexic children receive enriched language experience. Many of the traditional specialised approaches are very much what can be described as bottom-up approaches. That is, they deal to a great extent on the individual sub-skills of reading. It is, of course, these sub-skills, such as recognising and using phonemes, segmentation, letter sequence and letter and word recognition as well as the perceptual skills needed for letter recognition and formation that can provide considerable difficulties for dyslexic children. Unfortunately, it is all too easy to spend a disproportionate amount of time on these skills and this may result in the neglect of vital language experience.

Language experience can be achieved through discussion and approaches such as paired reading described later in this chapter. It is important that even if the child cannot access the print content of some books, the language, concepts and narratives should be discussed. This helps to make literacy motivating and emphasises the view that literacy is more than just reading. Literacy embraces many of the social conventions in society and is a powerful tool for social awareness, essential for young people when they leave school. Literacy also has a powerful cognitive component and can help to develop thinking skills in young children as long as reading is seen as much more than accuracy. That is one of the reasons why the experience of extended language and language concepts are important even though the child may not have that level of reading accuracy.

The books that are described by publishers as being of high interest and with a lower level of vocabulary can be excellent for developing both comprehension and reading fluency. Some examples of these are shown below.

High-interest books

The Hi-Lo readers from LDA, Cambridge and other similar books such as those from Barrington Stoke Ltd, Sandeman House, Trunk's Close, 55 High Street, Edinburgh, EH1 1SR, can be beneficial in relation to motivation. These books, particularly those from Barrington Stoke, have been written with the reluctant reader in mind and they can help children with dyslexia with reading fluency and also help in the development of reading comprehension and reading speed.

High-interest books – history

The BBC Education Scotland Series, published by Hodder Wayland, on history books for primary-aged children written by Richard Dargie, provide an excellent and stimulating source for reluctant readers. The books are on popular topics such as the Vikings and the Romans and include colourful illustrations, written in clear text with added features such as date timelines and glossaries, both of which are useful for children with dyslexia.

Start-to-Finish books

The series Start-to-Finish books (Don Johnston, 18 Clarendon Court, Calver Road, Winwick Quay, Warrington, WA2 8QP. Tel: 01925 241642; fax: 01925 241745 www.donjohnston.com) can be beneficial as the series, intended to boost reading and comprehension skills, provides a reader profile, a computer book, audiocassette and paperback book. Designed to engage children in reading real literature, the series can help with fluency and motivation. Some of the topics included in the series are: history, famous people, sports, original mysteries and retellings of classic literature. Don Johnston also produces some excellent software for children with literacy difficulties. This includes Write:OutLoud3. This program supports each step of the writing process including:

- *generating ideas* – helps with brainstorming and researching topics;
- *expressing ideas* – this allows children to hear their words as they write;
- *editing work* – using a spellchecker designed to check for phonetic misspellings; and
- *revising for meaning* – helps with word finding and improves written expression.

Differentiated texts

An example of this is the series of differentiated texts by Hodder-Wayland. They produce a series of books with two books on each of the themes covered. These texts which cover history topics, such as World War Two, geography topics, such as floods, the world's continents, and other diverse topics covering energy and cultural festivals. The differentiated text differs in that it has a reduced text length, more open page layout, bullet points to help with accessing information, clear type-face, captions in different print from the main text and the glossary and index use more simplified vocabulary from the text which is not differentiated.

Creative writing

Creative writing should, in fact, be one of the strengths displayed by dyslexic children. Often, of course, it is not. They may show difficulties with structure, sequencing the story, putting their point across and general grammar, syntax and punctuation.

It is important, therefore, to ensure that dyslexic children are provided with a clear structure so they know how they may embark on the task. They may know a great deal of detail about the topic they are writing on, but the difficulties associated with structure and also word retrieval can lead to a stilted and less elaborate account that will not reflect their actual level of knowledge of the topic. See David Wray's website for examples of writing frames:
www.warwick.ac.uk/staff/d.j.wray/ideas/frames.html

Supporting a task

Some other suggestions that can support the writing task are shown below – the example used below requires the child to write about their favourite football game or any other sport or hobby they are interested in.

Structure

- Key words – it is crucial that the key words are provided. Therefore, if the task is to write on a football game the following words need to be supplied and additionally it should be ensured, before the child embarks on the task, that they have an appropriate understanding of these words. This pre-task discussion will ensure the child has an understanding of the key words, ideas and concepts relating to the task.
- For the task above the key words may include the following:

– match ball	– linesman	– substitute
– referee	– excitement	– turf
– captain	– off–side	– half-time
– spectators	– foul play	– ball boy
– goalposts	– caution	– tactics
– score	– manager	– television cameras

- It is important that the learner has a good grasp of these words and ideas before embarking on the writing process. These words can also be presented in a mind map$^{©}$ form or with drawings or symbols next to each of the words. The advantage of a mind map$^{©}$ is that it also helps to organise the information into groups and additionally can facilitate a degree of creativity. (See later in this chapter.)

Sequence

The sequence is important as it allows the written work to flow and in fact make sense to the reader. Some children with dyslexia have difficulty knowing what to put first and often skip the introduction. Particular attention with introductions is time well spent.

Introduction

- Set the scene – brief description of the event, who, what, where and when and the importance of it.
- Outline of written work – then provide an outline of how you are going to describe the event, indicating some of the key words or phrases by highlighting their importance.

Main part

- The sequence of events – what happened first, then next and how did the event finish. This should be divided into paragraphs. There may also be a paragraph on half-time reflections.

Conclusion

- Summing-up – this would include the final details of the game, the thoughts of the managers and the spectators. Your own reflection on the event.

Grammar

It may be necessary for someone to help the dyslexic person with proof-reading. A useful suggestion is for the child to read it out aloud – if that is possible – as this can help identify any grammatical and syntactical errors. If proofreading is not possible then the student must certainly have additional time to check over his/her own work. Ideally if the written piece can be wordprocessed this would enhance the presenta-tion. Another advantage of wordprocessing the finished product is the spell check and grammar check software that is available in most wordprocessors. Two examples of such software are shown below.

Examples of software to support writing (see also Chapter 3).

TextHelp©

The program known as TextHelp© is particularly useful for assisting with writing. TextHelp© has a read-back facility and has a spellchecker that includes a dyslexic spell-check option that searches for common dyslexic errors. Additionally, TextHelp© has a word prediction feature that can predict a word from the context of the sentence giving up to ten options from a drop down menu. Often dyslexic students have a word-finding difficulty and this feature can be very useful. This software also has a 'word wizard' that provides the user with a definition of any word, options regarding homophones, an outline of a phonic map and a talking help file.

Kidspiration/Inspiration

Kidspiration/Inspiration are software programs that help the learner develop ideas and organise thinking. Through the use of diagrams the student is helped to comprehend words, concepts and information. Essentially the use of diagrams can help with the creating and modifying of concept maps and makes the organisation of ideas easier. The learner can also prioritise and rearrange his/her ideas. These programs can, therefore, be used for brainstorming, organising, prewriting, concept mapping, planning and outlining. In Inspiration, which is for age nine to adult, (Kidspiration is for children below nine), there are 35 in-built templates, and these can be used for a range of subjects including English, history and science. Dyslexic individuals often think in pictures rather than words. This technique can be used for note taking, for remembering information and organising ideas for written work. The Inspiration program converts this image into a linear outline.

Teacher modelling

Wray (2002) suggests that teacher modelling can be useful in developing reading and writing skills. He describes the background to shared reading and the approaches relating to metacognitive modelling as a way of teachers demonstrating to children the monitoring strategies they use in their own reading. He strongly advocates that teachers should model mental processes (what they think as they read or write) rather than procedures (what they do). Only in this way can children learn strategies that they can apply across a range of situations rather than merely being limited to the context in which they were encountered. Wray argues that the real benefits of shared reading, result not just from a teacher reading aloud to a group of learners, but from his/her thinking aloud at the same time.

This approach and shared writing are powerful teaching strategies and involve much more than just writing down what children say, acting as competent secretary to their authors. Wray suggests that shared writing provides teachers opportunities to:

- work with the whole class, to model, explore and discuss the decisions that writers make when they are writing;
- make links between reading and writing explicit;
- demonstrate how writers use language to achieve particular effects;

- remove temporarily some of the problems of orchestrating writing skills by taking on the burden of some aspects, for example, spelling and handwriting, thereby enabling the children to focus exclusively on how composition works;
- focus on particular aspects of the writing process, such as planning, composing, revising or editing;
- 'scaffold' children (see reference later in this chapter) in the use of appropriate technical language to discuss what writers do and think.

This can be extremely beneficial for dyslexic children and can help to promote the metacognitive awareness that they sometimes find challenging. Additionally, it incorporates them more fully into the work of the whole class.

Self-questioning

It is important that dyslexic children are encouraged and taught self-questioning. This will promote an enhanced awareness of the learning process. Learners who are explicitly taught a self-questioning procedure to accompany their reading are usually better able to identify inconsistencies and errors in texts (that is, monitor their comprehension) than other children who were directly told to look for these inconsistencies. Wray (2002) describes the self-questioning procedure these children were trained to apply. These consisted of the following questions, which they had to ask themselves as they read:

- First, I am going to decide if this story has any problems in it, like if one sentence says one thing and another sentence says something different or opposite.
- Second, as I read I will ask myself, 'Is there anything wrong with the story?'
- Third, I will read two sentences and stop and ask if anything is wrong.
- Fourth, so far, so good, I am doing a great job. Now I will read the whole story and decide if there are any problems in the whole story.
- Did I find any problems in this story?

Although children with dyslexia may have difficulty in reading fluently it is important that top-down and metacognitive approaches such as those described above are utilised. Essentially, one of the aims of education for children with dyslexia is the promotion of self-sufficiency in learning. The above strategies can help to do this. ·

Critical literacy

Literacy means more than reading – a broader view of literacy implies that the reader is able to comprehend the messages in the text, some of which may not be explicitly stated by the writer, but arrived at by inference on the part of the reader. 'Critical literacy' is a term used which challenges assumptions that texts can ever convey 'objective meanings' or that literacy is an ideologically neutral tool. According to Hunt (2002) critical literacy asserts that both readers and writers approach texts in ways that are conditioned by such factors as purpose, power relations, gender and historical period. The implication for teachers is that they need to do more than simply train children to become skilled decoders as the reading process needs to incorporate text participation (working out what the text means), text use ('knowing how to use the text in the immediate context) and text analysis (recognising how the text has been constructed to produce specific effects on the reader). In order to become independent readers children need to be explicitly aware of these dimensions, questioning the choices and assumptions that underlie the writer's words. From a 'critical literacy' perspective, literacy is not only seen as a neutral set of skills, but as social practice that is not necessarily empowering unless it is informed by critical awareness. It is important, therefore, that children with dyslexia are not rooted into tedious instruction and practice in decoding which would mean that the higher order skills implied in critical literacy are neglected.

The goal of literacy teaching is, therefore, the empowerment of the reader. Hunt suggests the following characteristics are common and readers need to be aware of these:

- a recognition that texts are constructed in specific ways in order to influence the reader;
- an emphasis on collaborative investigation of texts, rather than on individual reconstruction through reading aloud, comprehension exercises or appreciative response;
- encouragement of multiple interpretations rather than a quest for definitive meaning; and
- a commitment to social action; for example by writing in support of, or against, disputed texts, contacting authors and publishers, creating alternative versions, engaging in further research about issues raised.

According to Hunt some questions that can be raised by the reader can include:

- What themes are being used in the text?
- Who is the author writing for?
- Whose voices and positions are being expressed?
- Whose voices and positions are not being expressed?
- What is the text trying to do to you?
- What other ways are there of writing about the topic?
- What wasn't said about the topic? Why?

Using a critical literacy approach can provide the stimulation and the investigative experience that is necessary to develop language and learning skills and it is important that these aspects are not neglected in the teaching of children with dyslexia.

Other support approaches

Some other approaches that can be adapted from individualised programmes and used to support the classroom work are briefly described below. These approaches can readily be adapted and utilised within curriculum frameworks such as the Literacy Hour.

Multi-sensory Teaching System for Reading (MTSR)
This is a well-evaluated programme. The programme was designed to promote phonological awareness, ensure overlearning and to give time for review and attainment mastery. It is based on cumulative, structured, sequential, multisensory delivery with frequent small steps. The authors (Johnson, Phillips and Peer, 1999) conducted a research study into the use of the programme and found, as well as the above, it also encourages independent learning and improves self-esteem.

Phonological awareness approaches
There is strong evidence to suggest that phonological factors are of considerable importance in reading (Rack, 1994; Wilson and Frederickson, 1995; Snowling, 2000). Children with decoding problems appear to be considerably hampered in reading because they are unable to generalise from one word to another. This means that every word they read is unique, indicating that there is a difficulty in learning and applying phonological rules in reading. This emphasises the importance of teaching sounds/phonemes and ensuring that the child has an awareness of the sound/letter correspondence. Learning words by sight can enable some children to reach a certain standard in reading, but prevents them from adequately tackling new words and extending their vocabulary.

If children have a phonological awareness difficulty they are more likely to guess the word from the first letter cue and not the first sound, i.e. the word 'KITE' will be tackled from the starting point of the letter 'K' and not the sound 'ki' so the dyslexic reader may well read something like 'KEPT'. It is important, therefore, that beginning readers receive some structured training in the grapheme/phoneme correspondence; this is particularly necessary for dyslexic children who would not automatically, or readily, appreciate the importance of phonic rules in reading.

Phonological awareness procedures

The useful and easily accessible series of activities to promote phonological awareness (Gorrie and Parkinson, 1995) also begins with an assessment section. Following this, the remainder of the programme is in the form of game activities designed to develop specific areas of phonological development. For example, there are game activities on syllable segmentation, rhyme judgement, rhyme production, alliteration, onset and rime and phoneme segmentation. These games provide an excellent resource for the teacher and are suitable for children at different stages of phonological development.

Phonic Code Cracker

Phonic Code Cracker is a set of materials sub-divided into twelve units, each unit covering a different aspect of teaching literacy, for example Unit 3 deals with initial and final consonant blends, Unit 5 deals with common word endings and Unit 9 deals with common silent letters.

Phonic Code Cracker (Russell, 1993, revised 2000) is a very comprehensive and teacher-friendly set of materials. The scheme has been devised to provide intensive phonic practice for children who have been having difficulty acquiring basic literacy skills. It has been successfully used with children with specific reading difficulties in mainstream primary and secondary schools.

Essentially the scheme consists of support material and can be successfully used in combination with other schemes. Precision teaching methods are used, but no timescale is recommended as the author acknowledges that each child will have a different rate of learning. Assessment of the pupil's progress is measured through the use of pupil record skills. There are also fluency tests, time targets, accompanying computer software and – very important for building self-esteem – a mastery certificate which the child can retain as a record of his/her achievement.

Assisted learning

Assisted learning approaches are essentially teaching approaches that require considerable interaction between the learner and the teacher or other learners. This interaction may take the form of some kind of participant modelling. There may be an element of repetition and even simplicity in these approaches but, based on the principles of modelling and of facilitating the learning process, they can be successfully utilised with reading, writing and spelling.

Paired reading, peer tutoring, cued spelling and the apprenticeship approach to reading are examples of this kind of approach. Metacognitive approaches can also come under this category as such approaches can be based on interaction between teacher and student and this interaction can help the student acquire concepts and knowledge of the learning process. Metacognitive approaches will be dealt with in the following chapter. As an example of assisted learning, paired reading is described and discussed below.

Paired reading

Paired reading may be particularly useful for children with dyslexia since it provides both visual and auditory input simultaneously. It is a relatively straightforward technique that focuses on the following:

- parent and child reading together;
- programme to be carried out consistently;
- child selects reading material;
- as few distractions as possible;
- use of praise as re-inforcement; and
- discussion of the story and pictures.

The two principal stages of paired reading are – reading together and reading alone.

Reading together is when the parent/teacher and child read all the words aloud, with the adult adjusting the speed so that the pair read in harmony. The adult does not allow the child to become stuck at a word and if this happens will simply say the word to the child. This process, together with discussion, can help the child obtain meaning from the text and therefore enjoy the experience of language and of reading.

Reading alone occurs when the child becomes more confident at reading aloud. The adult can either read more softly, thus allowing the child to take the lead, or remain quiet. This can be done gradually to allow the child's confidence to build up (Topping, 1996). When the child stumbles at this stage, the adult immediately offers the word and then continues reading with the child again, until he/she gains enough confidence to read unaided.

Engaging parents

Mittler (2001) outlines the potential role for parents as children's first educators in the area of literacy acquisition and the respect that should be accorded to this role by schools. He suggests when parents and practitioners work together, particularly in the early years settings, the results have a positive impact on the child's development and learning. It is important therefore, and particularly for children at risk of dyslexia, that effective partnerships with parents are developed.

This means that a two-way flow of information, knowledge and expertise should be encouraged. Programmes such as paired reading can help with this. There are other programmes where the parent has a more instrumental role such as Toe by Toe.

Toe by Toe, A Highly Structured Multi-sensory Manual for Teachers and Parents (Cowling and Cowling, 1998)

This is a multi-sensory teaching method highly recommended for teachers and parents. The programme has a multi-sensory element, a phonic element and some focus on the student's memory through the planning and the timing of each of the lessons in the book. It can be readily used by parents and the instructions are very clear. The same author also has published a programme called 'Stride Ahead – An Aid to Comprehension' which can be a useful follow up to 'Toe by Toe'. Essentially 'Stride Ahead' has been written for children who can read but may have difficulty in understanding what they are reading.

Pause, Prompt, Praise

The programme Pause, Prompt, Praise (Glynn and McNaughton, 1985) was initially designed to be used with parents of pupils experiencing difficulties in literacy acquisition. The initial research work for Pause, Prompt, Praise was carried out in South Auckland, New Zealand, in home settings with a group of pupils and their parents. Subsequent research was carried out in the UK with the procedures of Research Monograph being published in the UK under the title Pause, Prompt, Praise (McNaughton et al, 1987). The Pause, Prompt, Praise strategies are derived from the theoretical perspective on reading developed by Clay (1985). It is based on the whole-book approach to the teaching of reading. Differences between proficient and poor readers are seen to lie in the flexibility with which they combine knowledge and letter-sound combinations with contextual information. Pause, Prompt, Praise is designed for use with individual pupils in order to facilitate opportunities to self-correct errors and practise strategies for problem-solving. McNaughton, Glynn and Robinson (1987) found that pausing before correction leads to a greater degree of self-correction by the learner and an increase in reading accuracy.

Learning strategies

Reciprocal teaching and scaffolding

Reciprocal teaching and scaffolding are both viewed as metacognitive strategies and, therefore, aim to promote self-sufficiency in learning. Reciprocal teaching refers to a procedure which both monitors and enhances comprehension by focusing on processes relating to questioning, clarifying, summarising and predicting (Palincsar and Brown, 1984). This is an interactive process and one that can help enhance the thinking and problem-solving skills of children with dyslexia. Brown (1993) describes the procedure for reciprocal teaching as one that is initially led by the teacher. The teacher leads the discussion by asking questions and this generates additional questions from participants. The questions are then clarified by teacher and participants together. The discussion is summarised by the teacher or participants, and a new 'teacher' is selected by the participants to lead the discussion on the next section of the text.

Scaffolding

'Scaffolding' describes the series of supports that can be built through teacher-pupil interaction to develop the understanding of text. This can be in the form of the teacher either providing the information or generating appropriate responses through questioning and clarifying. The supports are then withdrawn gradually, when the learner has achieved the necessary understanding to continue with less support.

Cudd and Roberts (1994) observed that poor readers were not automatically making the transfer from book language to their own writing. As a result, the students' writing lacked the precise vocabulary and varied syntax that was evident during reading. To overcome this difficulty Cudd and Roberts introduced a scaffolding technique to develop both sentence sense and vocabulary. They focused on sentence expansion by using vocabulary from the children's readers and using these as sentence stems which encouraged sentence expansion. Thus, the procedure used involved:

- selection of vocabulary from basal reader;
- embedding this vocabulary into sentence stems;
- selecting particular syntactic structures to introduce the stem;
- embedding the targeted vocabulary into sentence stems to produce complex sentences;
- discussing the sentence stems, including the concepts involved;
- completing a sentence using the stems;
- repeating the completed sentence providing oral reinforcement of both the vocabulary and the sentence structure; and
- encouraging the illustration of some of their sentences, helping to give the sentence a specific meaning.

Cudd and Roberts have found that this sentence expansion technique provides a 'scaffold' for children to help develop their sentence structure and vocabulary. Preliminary examination of writing samples of the students has revealed growth in vocabulary choice and sentence variety. The children, including those with reading and writing difficulties, were seen to gain better control over the writing process and gained confidence from using their own ideas and personal experiences.

Role-play to foster understanding

There is a great deal of evidence supporting the benefits of pre-reading discussion for the enhancement of both comprehension and decoding of text. Brozo (2003) develops this theme by suggesting that pre-reading strategies should involve active role-play techniques. He suggests that role-play strategies can help to accomplish reading readiness. Therefore, before introducing new learning to children the teacher needs to consider how the story can be translated into relevant experiences for them. He suggests that the planning steps for role-play need careful attention and should include the teacher asking questions such as, 'What are the human forces behind the events, how can the story impact on people and how can the content be personalised for the class?' Role-play activities should also leave scope for pupils to utilise creativity so that the students can personalise the situation. This can help the pupils call to mind relevant prior knowledge, encourage student participation and provide the pupils with a purpose for exploring the new text and the new learning. This can be of considerable benefit for children with dyslexia as it can provide a framework for learning and help to clarify some of the key ideas of the new text.

Transfer of skills

Transfer of skills is important for all children but particularly dyslexic children, otherwise previous learning may not be fully utilised. Children with dyslexia should be encouraged to reflect on learning and to interact with other learners and with the teacher through the stages described by Palincsar and Brown (1984) – questioning, clarifying, summarising and predicting. In this way active learning can be facilitated and this will provide the student with a structured framework for effective learning.

Nisbet and Shucksmith (1986) describe one example of such a framework that focuses on 'preparation, planning and reflection'. Preparation looks at the goals of the current work and how these goals relate to previous work. Planning looks at the skills and information necessary in order to achieve these goals, and the reflection aspect assesses the quality of the final piece of work, asking such questions as, 'What did the children learn from the exercise and to what extent could the skills gained be transferred to other areas?'

This example displays a structure from which it is possible to plan and implement a learning skills programme, and at the same time evaluate its effectiveness in relation to the extent of transfer of knowledge and skills to other curricular areas.

The traditional view of teaching dyslexic children is based on a number of well-founded principles that suggest that dyslexic children would benefit from a teaching programme which is characterised by its multi-sensory, sequential, cumulative and structured nature. Often this type of programme is implemented on a one-to-one basis with considerable overlearning. While this procedure may be effective for those with a low baseline in literacy, it is suggested here that this can perform a disservice to many dyslexic children by overlooking metacognitive aspects of learning, potential in thinking skills and learning styles.

This is important as there is evidence that dyslexic children may have difficulty with the metacognitive aspects of learning (Tunmer and Chapman, 1996). This implies that they need to be shown how to learn and the connections and relationships between different learning tasks need to be highlighted. This essentially means the emphasis should not necessarily be on the content or the product of learning but the process, that is, how learning takes place. Metacognitive strategies such as those described above – scaffolding, role-play and reciprocal teaching can facilitate new learning by using strategies and rules from previous learning, thereby enhancing the efficiency of the task of learning. Metacognition has an important role in learning and can help to develop thinking skills and can enhance an awareness of the learning process and the utilisation of effective strategies when learning new material. The teacher then has a key role to play in assessing metacognitive awareness and supporting its development (Peer and Reid, 2001).

Assessing metacognitive awareness

Three key aspects to assessing metacognitive awareness are questions relating to self-assessment, self-monitoring and self-direction. In relation to self-assessment the teacher could examine the following:

When tackling a new task does the child demonstrate self-assessment by asking questions such as:

- Have I done this before?
- How did I tackle it?
- What did I find easy?
- What was difficult?

- Why did I find it easy or difficult?
- What did I learn?
- What do I have to do to accomplish this task?
- How should I tackle it?
- Should I tackle it the same way as before?

In self-direction the following factors can be examined:

- Is the learner able to direct his/her own learning?
- Are they aware of the expectations of the task?
- How much time should they spend on the task?

Self-monitoring refers to the ability of the learner to monitor his/her own progress and to recognise if they are on the right track or not.

The above questions can help the learner be more aware of his/her own learning process and this is essential for children with dyslexia.

The use of metacognitive strategies can also help to develop reading comprehension and expressive writing skills. This can include:

- *Visual imagery* – discuss and sketch images from text.
- *Summary sentences* – identify the main ideas in text.
- *Webbing* – the use of concept maps of the ideas from a text.
- *Self-interrogation* – ask questions about what learners already know about a topic and what they may be expected to learn from the new passage.

Paired thinking

Topping (2002) suggests that teaching thinking skills can facilitate deep processing of information from text. Paired thinking is a framework for pairs working together. Some difference in reading ability is needed in each pair. The pairs can be:

- peers of the same or different ages;
- parents working with children at home;
- teaching assistants working with children in school; or
- volunteer adults (such as senior citizens) working with children in school.

Topping suggests that paired thinking is:

- very active and interactive – both the helper and the helped child are busy thinking all the time;
- low-cost to implement – in teacher time and other resources;

- socially inclusive – all children have an opportunity to participate;
- flexible – adaptive to a great variety of different neighbourhood, school and classroom contexts, and pupils of a wide range of ability; and
- durable – remaining to some extent effective when less than perfectly implemented or disrupted by pupil and teacher absence or other factors.

Paired thinking can provide:

- interactive cognitive challenge for both partners;
- practice in critical and analytic thinking, opportunities for scaffolding;
- praise and other social reinforcement;
- enables the pair to pursue their own interests and motivations;
- encourages critical and analytic discussion in the pair's vernacular vocabulary; and
- encourages self-disclosure of faulty or deficient thinking.

Paired thinking includes reading, listening, thinking, feeling and communicating. It also aims to help pupils to identify, review and evaluate the values they and others hold, and recognise how these affect thoughts and actions.

Topping provides very detailed procedures for paired thinking (Topping, 2002, in Reid and Wearmouth, 2002) that include teacher prompt sheets to support paired thinking activities. Topping outlines four levels that are intended to enable the teacher to differentiate and individualise the thinking activities for different pairs progressively. The fourth level can include aspects such as prediction, inference, deduction, intentionality, uncertainty, causality and evidence. Topping suggests that paired thinking can be easily incorporated into the literacy hour.

Multiple intelligences

The multiple intelligences concept, developed originally by Gardner (1983), involves eight intelligences. Gardner accepts that intelligences do not work in isolation but are usually interactive and combine with other intelligences, and where one differs from another is in the combination and how that combination works for the learner. Gardner suggests that everyone possesses these intelligences in some combination and all have the potential to use them productively. This has clear implications for the classroom and for children with dyslexia as they will possess these intelligences, perhaps in a different combination from some others, but will have the same potential to develop these in classroom activities. It is important, therefore, that the notion of multiple intelligences is incorporated into the teaching and learning process in schools.

The eight intelligences
The eight intelligences can be summarised as follows:

- verbal/linguistic – this involves language processing;
- logical/mathematical – which is associated with scientific and deductive reasoning;
- visual/spatial – deals with visual stimuli and visual planning;
- bodily/kinaesthetic – involves the ability to express emotions and ideas in action such as drama and dancing;
- musical/rhythmic – is the ability to recognise rhythmic and tonal patterns;
- interpersonal intelligence – involves social skills and working in groups;
- intrapersonal – involves metacognitive type activities and reflection; and
- naturalist intelligence – which relates to one's appreciation of the natural world around us, the ability to enjoy nature and to classify, for example, different species of flora and how we incorporate and react emotionally to natural environmental factors, such as flowers, plants and animals.

Each of the eight intelligences can be incorporated into teaching and curriculum development. This can be beneficial for children, such as dyslexic children, who may have a weakness in some aspects of language or other aspects of cognitive processing. This essentially turns the concept of deficits on its head and, as Gardner points out, every child has the potential for effective learning but their learning preferences and strengths need to be accessed. It is important, therefore, that the skills and preferences of children with dyslexia are utilised into a multiple intelligences curriculum. Lazear (1999) has made considerable effort to highlight the potential of multiple intelligences within daily classroom activities.

For example the:

- verbal/lingustic mode can incorporate creative writing, poetry and storytelling;
- logical/mathematical involves logic and pattern games and problem-solving;
- visual/spatial can involve guided imagery, drawing and design;
- bodily/kinaesthetic involves drama, role-play and sports;
- musical/rhythmic incorporates classroom activities which can relate to tonal patterns and music performance;

- intrapersonal intelligence can involve classroom activities on thinking strategies, metacognition and independent projects; and
- naturalist intelligence can take the form of field work as well as projects on conservation, evolution and the observation of nature.

Multiple intelligences as a guide to classroom practice can be very helpful in ensuring that the curriculum and the learning and teaching provide the opportunity for the child to display and extend his/her natural abilities in many areas.

Study skills

Study skills are essential for dyslexic children. There is some evidence that dyslexic children require particular help in this area, principally due to their organisational difficulties. A well-constructed study skills programme, therefore, is essential and can do much to enhance concept development, metacognitive awareness, transfer of learning and success in the classroom.

Such programmes will vary with the age and stage of the learner. A study skills programme for primary children would be different from that which may help students cope with examinations at secondary level. Well-developed study skills at the primary stage can provide a sound foundation for tackling new material in secondary school and help equip the student for examinations. Some of the principal factors in a study skills programme which will be discussed in this section include the following:

- communication skills;
- transfer of knowledge and skills;
- mapping and visual skills; and
- memory skills.

In relation to study skills and memory training in particular, the resources by Learning Works®, Freepost, (SCE11716), 9 Barrow Close, Marlborough, Wiltshire, SN8 2YY, www.learning-works.org.uk, can be extremely useful.

One such resource called 'memory trainers' includes many techniques and games to enhance memory. These resources are embedded within inclusion and there are guides for teachers, managers and SENCOs on meeting children's needs in an inclusive setting.

Communication skills·

Some of the factors which influence such skills include:

- organisation
- sequencing
- schemata development (concepts)
- confidence and motivation

Organisation

Children with dyslexia may require help to organise their thoughts. A structure should therefore be developed to help encourage this. It may not be enough to ask children, for example on completion of a story, 'What was the story about?' They need to be provided with a structure in order to elicit correct responses. This helps with the organisation of responses (output) which in turn can help to organise learning through comprehension (input). A structure which the teacher might use to elicit organised responses may include:

- What was the title?
- Who were the main characters?
- Describe the main characters.
- What did the main characters try to do?
- Who were the other characters in the story?
- What was the story about?
- What was the main part of the story?
- How did the story end?

In this way a structure is provided for the learner to retell the story. Moreover, the learner will be organising the information into a number of components such as 'characters', 'story', 'conclusion'. This will not only make it easier for the learner to retell orally, but will help to give him/her an organisational framework which will facilitate the retention of detail. The learner will also be using a strategy which can be used in other contexts. This will help with the new learning and the retention of new material.

Sequencing

Dyslexic children may have some difficulty in retelling a story or giving information orally in the correct sequence. It is important that sequencing of information should be encouraged and exercises which help facilitate this skill can be developed. Thus, in the retelling of a story, children should be provided with a framework that can take account of the sequence of events. Such a framework could include:

- How did the story start?
- What happened after that?
- What was the main part?
- How did it end?

Various exercises, such as the use of games, can be developed to help facilitate sequencing skills.

Schemata development (concepts)

The development of schemata helps the learner organise and categorise information. It also ensures the utilisation of background knowledge. This can aid comprehension and recall.

When children read a story or a passage, they need to relate this to their existing framework of knowledge – i.e. their own schema. So when coming across new knowledge, learners try to fit it into their existing framework of knowledge based on previous learning, which is the schema they possess for that topic or piece of information. It is important for the teacher to find out how developed a child's schema is on a particular topic, before providing more and new information. Being aware of this will help the teacher ensure the child develops appropriate understanding of the new information. Thus, some key points about the passage could help the reader understand the information more readily and provide a framework into which the reader can slot ideas and meaning from the passage. Schemata, therefore, can help the learner:

- attend to the incoming information;
- provide a scaffolding for memory;
- make inferences from the passage which also aid comprehension and recall; and
- utilise his/her previous knowledge.

There are a number of strategies which can help in the development of schemata. An example of this can be seen in an examination of a framework for a story. In such a framework two principal aspects can be discerned:

- the structure of the story; and
- the details related to the components of the structure.

The structure of a story can be seen in the following components:

- background
- context
- characters
- beginning

- main part
- events
- conclusion

Background knowledge

Background knowledge is an important aid to comprehension. It is suggested that background knowledge in itself is insufficient to facilitate new learning, but must be skilfully interwoven with the new material that is being learnt. It is important that the learner is able to use the new information in different and unfamiliar situations. Hence the connections between the reader's background knowledge and the new information must be highlighted in order for the learner to incorporate the new knowledge in a meaningful manner.

The ideas contained in a text, therefore, must be linked in some way to the reader's background knowledge and the ideas need to be presented in a coherent and sequential manner. Such coherence and sequencing of ideas at the learning stage not only allows the material to be retained and recalled, but also facilitates effective comprehension. Being aware of the learner's prior knowledge of a lesson is, therefore, of fundamental importance. Before embarking on new material prior knowledge can be linked with the new ideas, in order to pave the way for effective study techniques and strategies to enhance comprehension and recall.

Memory skills

Children with dyslexic difficulties may have difficulties in remembering, retaining and recalling information. This may be due to working memory and short-term memory problems (BPS, 1999) or naming difficulty, particularly at speed, i.e. difficulty in recalling the name or description of something without cues (Wolf and O'Brien, 2001). It is important to encourage the use of strategies that may facilitate remembering and recall. Such strategies can include repetition and overlearning, the use of mnemonics and mind mapping[©].

Repetition and overlearning

Short-term memory difficulties can be overcome by repetition and rehearsal of materials. This form of overlearning can be achieved in a variety of ways and not necessarily through conventional, and often tedious, rote learning.

In order to maximise the effect of repetition of learning it is important that a multi-sensory mode of learning is utilised. Repetition of the material to be learned can be accomplished through oral, visual, auditory and kinaesthetic modes. The learner should be able to see, hear, say and touch the materials to be learned. This reinforces the input stimuli and helps to consolidate the information for use, meaning and transfer to other areas. There are implications here for multi-mode teaching, including the use of movement, perhaps drama, to enhance the kinaesthetic mode of learning.

Mnemonics

Mnemonics can be auditory or visual, or both auditory and visual. Auditory mnemonics may take the form of rhyming or alliteration while visual mnemonics can be used by relating the material to be remembered to a familiar scene, such as the classroom.

Mind mapping[©]

Mind mapping[©] was developed by Buzan to help children and adults develop their learning skills and utilise as much of their abilities as possible. The procedure is now widely used and can extend memory capacity and develop lateral thinking (Buzan, 1993). It can be a simple or a sophisticated strategy depending on how it is developed and used by the individual. It is used to help the learner to remember a considerable amount of information and encourages students to think of, and develop, the main ideas of a passage or material to be learned. It adopts in many ways some of the principles already discussed in relation to schemata theory.

Essentially mind maps are individual learning tools and someone else's mind map may not be meaningful to you. It is important, therefore, that children should create their own, in order to help with both understanding of key concepts and in the retention and recall of associated facts.

Mind mapping[©] can help not only to remember information, but also to help organise that information and this exercise in itself can aid understanding. Elaborate versions of mind maps can be constructed using pictorial images, symbols and different colours.

Comment

This chapter has focused on teaching and learning approaches that can be used for children with dyslexia. While there are a great number of specialised teaching approaches that are available, it is suggested in this chapter that knowledge of the individual learner as well as an understanding of the processes of learning are essential to help develop the skills of dyslexic children. It is important to recognise that dyslexia is more than a difficulty with reading, but involves other cognitive factors, such as short-term and long-term memory and processing speed, all of which can affect learning.

This emphasises the importance of metacognitive strategies and study skills. It is essential that the development of these skills is given a high priority in any programme of work for children with dyslexia as well as factors more directly related to reading, such as phonological awareness and language experience. The main aspects of these are:

- communication skills, which can be aided by organisation, sequencing, context, schema, confidence and motivation;
- the transfer of these skills to other areas of the curriculum;
- mapping and visual skills; and
- strategies in remembering and retention are all important.

These aspects can be developed with, and by, the learner. Although the teacher can help to facilitate these strategies and skills in the learner, it is still important that any skill or strategy that is developed is personalised by the learner. This means that different learners will adopt different ways of learning and remembering materials, but the responsibility to allow the learner to do this, and to understand the principles and strategies associated with study skills, rests with the teacher.

Chapter 3

Curriculum Perspectives and Planning for Learning

The difficulties that can be experienced by children with dyslexia are well documented. As indicated in previous chapters many of these difficulties arise from biological and cognitive factors, resulting in difficulties with information processing, particularly in relation to print and language, organisation and speed of processing. It is not surprising that many of the popular interventions relate to specialised programmes and specific strategies that focus on these difficulties, and attempt to help the child develop literacy, memory and learning skills. These approaches recognise that the 'within-child difficulties' may prevent effective learning and for that reason strategies and programmes are sought to deal with these difficulties.

There is no shortage of programmes to deal with these difficulties (see Reid, 2003, for a full description of many of these programmes). One of the drawbacks of these is that, by necessity, they often single out, or even isolate, children from others in the class. This can affect the child's self-esteem and, further, it may be at the cost of missing out on some aspects of the mainstream curriculum.

For these reasons it is essential to adopt a curriculum perspective to accompany any specific approaches that may be used. This means that the onus is on the teacher to prepare and present the curriculum in a dyslexia-friendly manner. This will require effective differentiation in the preparation of materials and these will need to consider classroom and environmental factors, such as learning styles and the classroom layout.

This chapter will examine and discuss interventions from a curricular and classroom perspective and highlight the importance of focusing, not only on the child, but the learning and teaching context.

Interventions and dyslexia

The debate
There is an ongoing debate regarding the 'special' type of teaching that is required for children with dyslexia. This debate is encapsulated in the views presented by Norwich and Lewis (2001). In this paper they question the claims that differential teaching is required for children with special educational needs, including dyslexia. They claim that the

'unique differences position' (p. 313) which suggests that differentiated teaching is needed for this group has little supportive empirical evidence and in fact are adaptations to common teaching approaches. (A fuller discussion of this is provided in Lewis and Norwich, 2004.) Conner (1994) argues that specialist teaching approaches for dyslexia are little different from teaching literacy to any pupil, although arguably there seems to be more of a preference to bottom-up approaches relating to phonological awareness as well as structure and overlearning. Reason *et al.* (1988) also questions the differences in specialist approaches, indicating that individual differences within the dyslexic students are the most crucial factor in relation to utilising specific teaching approaches. Given this controversy and debate it may be more productive to identify specific approaches by examining the barriers to learning experienced by the child. This would imply that each child is individual and the specific barriers may be different for different children. One way of dealing with this is through the use of individual education plans. These can identify the barriers to learning and identify strategies and approaches to overcome these barriers and contextualise them within the learning and classroom situation.

Individual Education Plans (IEPs) – implications for children with dyslexia

Individual Education Plans can provide a means of ensuring the needs of children are met within the educational setting. In fact since the publication of the 'Code of Practice for the Identification and Assessment of Special Educational Needs' (DfEE, 1994), the IEP has become a major tool for planning individual pupils' programmes of study in England, Wales and Northern Ireland and are also used to some extent in Scotland and the Republic of Ireland. The term 'Individual Education Plan' can be used to refer to both the process of planning the next steps in a pupil's learning programme on the basis of an analysis of pupil needs and the summative document (Tod, Castle and Blamires, 1998) used to record the IEP. In the Republic of Ireland, this can also be referred to as the Individual Profile and Learning Programme.

Individual education plans

It is important to ensure that IEPs are developed and used appropriately. Some criticism of IEPs has been noted by Macintyre and Deponio (2003) who cite evidence from Scotland (Scottish Executive, 2002) which suggests that consultation during the development of IEPs, particularly with parents and children, is lacking.

However, with full consultation, IEPs can be invaluable and can provide both day-to-day information on specific performances, as well as more medium and long-term targets.

In order for an IEP to be used appropriately it should at least contain the following:

- details of the nature of the child's learning difficulties;
- the special educational provision to be made;
- strategies to be used;
- specific programmes, activities, materials;
- any specialised equipment;
- targets to be achieved;
- the time frame for any specified targets;
- monitoring and assessment arrangements; and
- review arrangements with dates.

An example of an IEP for a child with dyslexia is shown below.

HIGH SCHOOL – Individual Education Plan

(Reproduced with permission of F. Renaldi, Support for Learning Teacher)

Name: **Class:** **Timescale:** December 03–March 04

Pupil profile: Is a friendly, sociable pupil. However, this hides some issues of his reluctance to come into school during his primary years and also in secondary. He has found the adjustment into secondary school hard at times with peer issues of bullying and coming to terms with the workload. Pupil Support has worked with him on these issues and he does appear to be more settled and happy.

Strengths: Has good ideas, converses well, and is happy to accept help. He is coping well with his awareness that he has a different learning style and requirements than some of his classmates.

Needs: Concentrate on good behaviour and finishing the tasks set. Try to be organised and faster in getting ready for a lesson.

Recommendations from last annual review:
- Contact LS department for more details and help
- Encourage pupil to take part in discussions.
- Accept other methods of evidence for pupils learning.

SfL support strategies:
- In class support for Maths, English, History, French, Geography.
- Support in provision of a differentiated curriculum using multi sensory strategies, audio tapes, work sheets,
- IT support – success maker.
- Home work club
- Paired reader program

Pupil's targets: carried over from last review
- Organised for school – different folders for each subject.
- Become familiar with keyboard in order to present work for teachers.
- Try to behave in class and not get distracted – leave tie alone
- Improve attainment in maths and spelling.
- To join a school club.

Action:
Teachers should:
• Contact LS department for more details and help
• Encourage pupil to take part in discussions.
• Accept other methods of evidence for pupils learning.

SfL support strategies:
• In class support for Maths, English, History, French, Geography.
• Support in provision of a differentiated curriculum using multi sensory strategies, audio tapes, work sheets,
• IT support – success maker.

SfL support strategies: Subject specific.

Maths – In class support and withdrawal 1 Period to work on basic maths skills. Currently working on time, measurement and algebra. 1 P per week on Success maker – maths program (this has come from the French lessons)

English – In class support. Audio tapes of novels and plays are provided. He is to listen to these before the lesson at home – particularly the Midsummer Nights dream. The cartoon version of the play has been shown to the whole class and the play has also been read out loud. He had an opportunity to take a part which he volunteered for – Lysander, however he decided not to continue. The pupils in the class all have swapped roles.

French – Modern languages have proven to be a difficult area. However he has 4 periods of in-class support and the presentation of the lesson is multi sensory also using small mime games. These tasks he enjoys, however, there are concerns about the longer-term accessibility of the curriculum. He is working on a lower level text booklet – Heinemann French which does seem to be running along side the rest of the classes material, although it is not ideal. He likes this subject even though 'he does not understand it'. A conversational French programme may be more suitable.

History – There is a relatively large amount of reading in this subject, however, the support for learning is putting on to audio tape material for the next topics – Stonehenge and then the Romans.
The history tests are being re written/presented in a more dyslexia friendly format for all pupils. Key spellings are also being gathered.

Achievement criteria:
• Pass a level C maths test.
• Able to answer questions & tasks on "Google Eyes" in English

Achieved (date)
Working within level D. Achieved all tasks. Nov 03

Not achieved Still working on. Dec 03

Parental involvement:
• Maintain contact with school. Feel free to contact LS teacher if concerned or if something is not working.
• Attended regular review meetings
• Oversee homework and study
• Continue to be positive.

Evaluation
The strategies appear to be working. He is trying to complete Home works, however does 'turn off' during lessons if the differentiation is not in place.
Additional support has been put into operation for French.

Planning for learning in the primary school

In many schools the class teacher can be supported by learning support staff and special educational needs co-ordinators, but essentially the responsibility for planning and preparing classwork does rest with the class teacher. It is important, therefore, that class teachers have some awareness of dyslexia, but equally it is important that consideration is given to the role of planning and preparation in meeting the needs of dyslexic children, within the class and curriculum context.

Planning, presentation and materials

Planning for learning should include consultation, how the information is presented as well as how materials and tasks are developed. There are many fundamental factors that can be incorporated into the planning and presentation of curricular materials and tasks. These include the following:

Planning

- Knowledge of the child's strengths and difficulties – this is essential, especially since not all children with dyslexia will display the same profile. This is therefore the best starting point as often strengths can be used to help deal with the weaknesses.
- For example, dyslexic children often have a preference for visual and kinaesthetic learning and a difficulty with auditory learning. Therefore phonics, which relies heavily on sounds, and the auditory modality, need to be introduced together with visual and experiential forms of learning. The tactile modality, involving touch and feeling the shape of letters that make specific sounds, should also be utilised, as well as the visual symbol of these letters and letter/sound combinations. Programmes such as Letterland (Wendon, 1987) can be useful as this type of programme, by using pictograms, introduces the sound in a meaningful, visual and kinaesthetic manner.
- Consultation – the responsibility for dealing with children with dyslexia within the classroom should not rest solely with the class teacher. Ideally it should be seen as a whole-school responsibility. This means that consultation with school management and other colleagues is important and, equally, it is important that time is allocated for this. Information from previous teachers, support staff, school management and parents are all important and such joint liaison can help to ensure the necessary collaboration to provide support for the class teacher. It is important that this should be built into the school procedures and not be a reaction to a problem that has occurred – such collaboration can be seen as preventative and proactive.

- Knowledge of the curriculum content – it is understood the teacher will have a sound awareness of the content of the curriculum that the child needs to know. Anticipating those areas for the different aspects of the curriculum that may present a difficulty for dyslexic children may, however, be a bit more tricky. Yet it is important that the teacher can anticipate those areas that may be problematic for dyslexic children.

Such areas can include information that contains lists or dates in, for example history. Learning the sequence of dates can be as difficult as remembering the dates. It is crucial, therefore, that such information is presented in a dyslexia-friendly manner and this requires a degree of preparation. A good example of how this can be done is shown in the figure below of a timeline. Information that corresponds to the dates can be placed alongside.

The Vikings in Scotland

TIMELINE

AD 400–800 the period sometimes known as the 'Dark Ages'

795 Viking longships make their first raid on the abbey of Iona

798 Vikings raid the Hebrides

825 Vikings attack Iona looking for the magical relics of St Columba and murder the abbot, St Blathmac

830–840 Norse settle in the Orkney and Shetland Islands

850 Norse settle in Sutherland and Caithness in north Scotland

866 Olaf leads a fleet of warriors from the Viking base of Dublin in Ireland to attack the west coast of Scotland

870 Dumbarton Rock in Strathclyde is besieged by Vikings

874 Harald Finehair leads his great fleet from Norway to police the Vikings on the Orkney Islands

894 Einar the Turf cutter becomes Jarl of the Orkney Islands

980–1050 many Norse in Scotland become Christian

1000 Sigurd the Fat rules as great Jarl

1014 Sigurd dies in the bloody battle of Clontarf in Ireland

1048 Jarl Thorfinn, travels as a pilgrim to visit the pope in Rome

1040–1065 the earldom of the Orkney Islands reaches its most powerful

1101 King Edgar of Scotland pays the Norse not to attack his land

1137 Jarl Rognvald begins building Saint Magnus Cathedral in Kirkwall

1151 Rognvald leads his men on a pilgrimage

1155 Somerled rules a kingdom in the western islands of Scotland

1164 Somerled dies attacking the town of Renfrew

1200 Scottish and Norwegian royal families intermarry

1225–1240 Snorri Turluson in Iceland writes down the Viking saga

1230 a Norse army captures the important castle of Rothesay

1263 King Haakon IV of Norway sails with a fleet of 150 ships to try and recapture his lands in Scotland. His army perishes in the siege of Largs

1266 King Magnus gives the Hebrides to the king of Scots

1468 Scandinavian rule ends in the Orkney Islands

1469 Scandinavian rule ends in the Shetland Islands

1700 the Norse language of Norn dies out in the Northern Isles

(reproduced from Dargie, *Vikings in Scotland*, with permission from Hodder Wayland)

The figure on the previous page helps us to view the main events in sequence – this can be made more accessible for children with dyslexia through the use of visuals to represent these key events. Visuals, such as diagrams, that represent these events can be provided by the teacher but it is often more effective to ask children to construct their own visual representations. This is likely to be more meaningful to them as it is their own particular image of the event. Other important factors include:

• Current level of literacy acquisition – an accurate and full assessment of the child's current levels of attainment is necessary in order to plan an effective programme of learning. The assessment should include listening comprehension as well as reading accuracy and fluency. Listening comprehension can often be a more accurate guide to the abilities and understanding of dyslexic children than reading and spelling accuracy. Indeed it is often the discrepancy between listening comprehension and reading accuracy that can be a key factor in identifying dyslexia. Information on the levels of attainment will be an instrumental factor in planning for differentiation.

• Cultural factors – similarly background knowledge, particularly cultural factors, are also important as these can influence selection of books and whether some of the concepts in the text need to be singled out for additional and differentiated explanation. Cultural values are an important factor. It has been suggested that the 'big dip' in performance noted in some bilingual children in later primary school may be explained by a failure of professionals to understand and appreciate the cultural values, and the actual level of competence of the bilingual child, particularly in relation to conceptual development and competence in thinking skills. According to Landon (1999) teachers may misinterpret bilingual children's development of good phonic skills in the early stages of literacy development in English and may in fact fail to note the difficulties that these children might be having with comprehension. When the difficulties later emerge, these children are grouped inappropriately with native-speakers of English who have the more conventional problems with phonic awareness, or their difficulties are assumed to derive from specific perceptual problems rather than from the cultural unfamiliarity of the text.

In order for a teaching approach with bilingual students to be fully effective it has to be comprehensive, which means that it needs to incorporate the views of parents and the community. This requires considerable preparation and pre-planning, as well as consultation with parents and community organisations.

Presentation

- Small steps – it is important, especially since children with dyslexia may have short-term memory difficulties, to present tasks in small steps. In fact one task at a time is probably sufficient. If multiple tasks have to be provided, then a checklist might be a useful way for the child to note and self-monitor his/her progress.

- Group work – it is important to plan for group work. The dynamic of the group is crucial and dyslexic children need to be in a group where at least one person in the group is able to impose some form of structure to the group tasks. This can act as a modelling experience for dyslexic children – it is also important that those in the group do not overpower the dyslexic child – so someone with the ability to facilitate the dyslexic child's contribution to the group is also important. This would make the dyslexic child feel they are contributing to the group. Although they may not have the reading ability of the others in the group, they will almost certainly have the comprehension ability, so will be able to contribute, if provided with opportunities.

- Learning styles – this is one of the key aspects in understanding the importance of presentation of materials and how the learning situation can be manipulated to promote more effective learning. It is important to recognise that different children will have their own preferred learning style and this includes dyslexic children. This means that there may be a great many similarities in how children with dyslexia learn and process information but there will also be individual differences and these need to be taken into account in the planning and presentation of learning.

As suggested earlier, multi-sensory strategies are used widely in the teaching of dyslexic children. The evidence suggests that the effectiveness of these strategies is based largely on the provision of at least one mode of learning with which the learner feels comfortable. Thus, if the learner has a difficulty dealing with information by way of the auditory channel, this could perhaps be compensated for through the use of the visual mode. The use of such compensatory strategies is well documented in the literature and is a feature of teaching programmes for dyslexic children. It is logical, therefore, that consideration of the learner as an individual should be extended to a holistic appreciation of the learner's individual style. Factors such as affective (emotional) and physiological characteristics will have some bearing on how the dyslexic child responds to the learning situation, and a holistic perspective should therefore be applied both in assessment and teaching of dyslexic children.

One of the most useful learning styles models is that developed by Dunn, Dunn and Price (1975–89). This model identifies five principal domains and 21 elements, all of which affect student learning. It is suggested that all these elements have to be considered during the assessment process and in subsequent planning of teaching. The five principal domains and the 21 elements across those domains are:

- environmental (sound, light, temperature, design);
- emotional (motivation, persistence, responsibility, structure);
- sociological (learning by self, pairs, peers, team, with an adult);
- physiological (perceptual preference, food and drink intake, time of day, mobility); and
- psychological (global or analytic preferences, impulsive and reflective).

On examining the above learning styles model, one can recognise how the elements identified can influence the performances of dyslexic learners. It must be appreciated that dyslexic learners are first and foremost learners, and like any other learners will be influenced by different learning conditions. Some dyslexic students therefore, will prefer a 'silent' environment for concentration while others may need some auditory stimuli, perhaps even music, in order to maximise concentration and performance. Similarly, with 'light' – individual preferences such as dim light and bright light should be recognised. In fact in relation to music Overy, Nicolson, Fawcett and Clarke (2001) reported on cognitive benefits in music training. They suggest that music training can be used as a multi-sensory medium for the development of timing skills, in which a strong emphasis can be placed on analytical listening and accurate motor skills.

In relation to emotional variables, two of the elements, responsibility and structure, should certainly be addressed. It has been well documented that dyslexic learners benefit from imposed structure – most of the teaching programmes recognise this and follow a highly structured formula. At the same time, however, taking responsibility for one's own learning can be highly motivating and can generate success – dyslexic learners should not be deprived of the opportunity to take responsibility for their learning as some may possess a natural preference for responsibility and structure.

Identification of learning style

It is possible to obtain some ideas of the child's learning style from observation and knowledge of how the child tackles tasks in the classroom. Some suggestions for this have been developed into a framework that highlights emotional, social, cognitive, physical, environmental and metacognitive factors. These are shown in some detail in Chapter 1 of this book.

Learning styles – key points

The key points in relation to learning styles are:

- Firstly, every effort should be made to organise the classroom environment in a manner which can be adapted to suit a range of styles.
- In classrooms where there are a number of dyslexic learners the environment should be global (Given and Reid, 1999). This means that the lighting, design and indeed the whole learning atmosphere need to be considered.
- It is also important that the teacher has an awareness of what is meant by learning styles and how to identify different styles in children.
- Although there are many different instruments that can be used, teachers' observations and discussion with students while they are engaged on a task can be extremely beneficial.
- The different stages of the information processing cycle (see below) can be considered in relation to how children learn and these factors can be used within a learning styles structure.
- The experience of learning may be more important to children with dyslexia than the actual finished product.
- At the same time it is important that children with dyslexia themselves become aware of their own learning style. This is the first and most important step to achieving a degree of self-sufficiency in learning. Acknowledging learning styles, therefore, can help to promote skills that extend beyond school. Knowledge of learning styles can equip students and particularly students with dyslexia for lifelong learning.

Knowledge of information processing

Learning depends on how efficiently and effectively children process information. It is important to recognise the key stages of information processing and how these may present potential difficulties for learners with dyslexia. Some of these difficulties are shown in Chapter 1 but it is important to recognise that these potential difficulties can be overcome with forward planning and recognition of these difficulties in the planning of teaching programmes and individual lessons. Some suggestions for this are shown below:

Information processing

Input
- Identify the students' preferred learning style, particularly visual, auditory, kinaesthetic or tactile preferences as these can be crucial in

how information is presented. It is important to present new information to the learners preferred modality.

- Present new information in small steps – this will ensure that the short-term memory does not become overloaded with information before it is fully consolidated.
- New material will need to be repeatedly presented through over-learning. This does not mean that the repetition should be in the same form – rather it is important that it should be varied using as wide a range of materials and strategies as possible.
- It is a good idea to present the key points at the initial stage of learning new material. This helps to provide a framework for the new material and can help to relate new information to previous knowledge.

Cognition

- Information should be related to previous knowledge. This ensures that concepts are developed and the information can be placed into a learning framework, or schema by the learner. Successful learning is often due to efficient organisation of information. It is important, therefore, to group information together and to show the connection between the two. For example, if the topic to be covered was the Harry Potter series of books, then concepts such as witchcraft and magic, and the words associated with these would need to be explained and some of the related ideas discussed. This should be done prior to reading the text.
- Some specific memory strategies, such as mind mapping© and mnemonics can be used to help the learner remember some of the key words or more challenging ideas. This can be done visually through mind mapping©.

Output

- Often children with dyslexia have difficulty identifying the key points in new learning or in a text. This can be overcome by providing the child with these key points or words at the beginning stage of learning the new material. Additionally the learner can acquire skills in this by practising using summaries. Each period of new learning should be summarised by the learner – this in itself helps to identify the key points.
- It may also be beneficial to measure progress orally, rather than in writing, particularly in-class continuous assessment. It is not unusual for children with dyslexia to be much more proficient orally than in written form. Oral presentation of information can therefore help to instil confidence. By contrast, often a written exercise can be damaging in terms of confidence, unless considerable preparation and planning have helped to ensure that some of the points indicated above are put in to place.

Materials

- Use of coloured paper – there is some evidence that different colours of background and font can enhance some children's reading and attention.
- Layout – the page layout is very important and this should be visual but not overcrowded. Coloured background is also usually preferable. Font size can also be a key factor and this should not be too small. In relation to the actual font itself it has been suggested that Sassoon, Comic Sans and Times New Roman are the most dyslexia-friendly fonts.

Planning for learning in the secondary school

Provision and practice

One of the key issues in relation to successful outcomes in secondary school concerns the notion of responsibility. It is important to ensure that the needs of dyslexic children are met and that all members of staff become fully involved.

School management need to ensure that:

- The ethos of the school is supportive. The philosophy of the school together with attitudes and actions are known to all staff including part-time support and other staff.
- All staff should be encouraged to acknowledge that with effective differentiation the curriculum can be accessed by dyslexic children.
- • All teaching staff need to be supported in order to utilise some of the suggestions shown above in relation to planning, presentation and the development of materials.
- Parents need to be considered. Parents are a very rich support of information and assistance and it is important that collaboration between home and school is ongoing (Reid, 2005).

Accessing subject content

It can be suggested that if the subject materials and teaching plans are developed and implemented in a manner that is compatible with the dyslexic student, the student should be able to perform on the same terms as his/her peers. Although most of the subject content is determined by examination considerations and prescribed curricular, much can still be done to identify the potential areas of the curriculum that may present difficulties for dyslexic students.

There is no reason, therefore, why the content of all subjects cannot be developed in a dyslexia-friendly manner. It can be argued that the principles for making information dyslexia-friendly are the same for every subject. The key to achieving this is forward-planning together with an awareness of dyslexia. This also implies an awareness of differentiation, learning styles and dyslexia-friendly assessment procedures.

Some examples of this are shown below for different subject areas of the curriculum.

English

In English it is important to use a range of sources, for example in literature, so that the dyslexic student can access a novel or play. It is often best to begin with discussion so that the overall story and plot can be understood before any reading begins. This also fits in with the learning style of many dyslexic students, as these appear to favour holistic processing as opposed to analytical. This means that the learner would need to understand the ideas and the background to the novel before reading it. This also helps to build concepts and schema. Schema essentially refers to the student's own understanding of a situation or an event. It is important that the student has an appropriate schema before commencing to read. Having a schema or framework will help the reader use context and understanding to help read difficult words, and indeed understand the novel without actually reading every word.

There are many aspects relating to English that can be challenging for students with dyslexia – expressive writing, spelling, grammar, as well as reading accuracy and fluency.

It is important to acknowledge the different types of reading activities and the different strategies that can be used for each. Reading examination questions and reading instructions will require a detailed and accurate form of reading. For the student with dyslexia this will mean that additional time will be necessary and they can produce a checklist to ensure they have understood the instructions. Such a list can include – What is actually being said/asked? What is required of me? How will I know if I am right? In other words the teacher is encouraging the student to think about the implications of the question/instructions and to consider the information gleaned in different ways. By doing this it should become apparent to the student, if the question has been misread.

Similarly, in reading for facts the reader can make a checklist of different types of information under different headings. It may also be helpful if the teacher actually provides the headings for the student. The student with dyslexia needs to obtain practice in scanning and reading to obtain a general overview or impression of the text. One way to practice scanning is to give the learner a passage to read, but not give them sufficient time to read the passage. This means they will be forced to read only the key words.

These factors emphasise the importance of forward planning and breaking challenging areas down into smaller components. This means that the teacher will be able to identify which of these aspects present the most challenges and then work through the range of strategies that can be used for these areas. Some of the strategies include those that can be used for good teaching in general – teaching in a multi-sensory manner, helping to boost the students memory through the use of mnemonics, personal spelling notebooks, the use of ICT to help with reading and the use of the Internet to investigate topics. It can sometimes be useful if the student with dyslexia can work in groups as he/she can share skills with others in the group. The reading part can be done by someone else in the group while the dyslexic person can deal with some of the other aspects of the task.

Geography

Geography is a subject that can be accessed by dyslexic students. It has the potential to be highly visual and the subject content relates to the study of people and activities in the community and world around us. In other words it is a subject that has direct relevance to living in today's world. This means that information in geography can be accessed in a variety of ways – field trips, visually, visits, interviews and observation, quite apart from using reading materials.

Additionally, the geography curriculum lays emphasis on the 'enquiry approach' in developing geographical knowledge and under-standing. This can be noted in the statement below.

'Geography develops knowledge of places and environments throughout the world, an understanding of maps, and a range of inves-tigative and problem-solving skills, both inside and outside the classroom. As such it prepares pupils for adult life and employment.' (DfEE and QCA, 1999)

In geography, as in many of the other subject areas, alternatives to the written answer can be used to a great extent. Students with dyslexia usually have skills in the visual/kinaesthetic areas as opposed to the auditory area. This means that they will learn more effectively by active learning through projects, field trips and interviews. They may also work well in groups. It is important to ensure that students with dyslexia can present their work in a variety of ways using multi-media, including tapes, videos and ICT.

It is important that geography is underpinned by understanding and this is why active participatory learning is essential for dyslexic learners. It is crucial that the skills and abilities of dyslexic students in the areas of visual processing and understanding are not restricted because of lack of access to print materials. It was interesting to note that in the interviews conducted by Williams and Lewis (2001) with dyslexic students studying geography, one of the recurrent themes reported by the students was the lack of opportunities to show their knowledge.

History

History is a subject that can be stimulating and engaging for the dyslexic student. It essentially demands investigation and skills in problem-solving, but too often the actual demands placed on the student relate to memory demands and the learning of massive amounts of facts. This of course need not be the case and it is necessary to consider ways how the student might acquire the necessary information without resorting to rote memorisation.

Dargie (2001) suggests that discussion holds the key to this. Talking through an issue, he suggests, can help pupils rehearse the separate components of a topic and develop an argument that they can then use in written work.

At the same time the student with dyslexia can develop his/her own timeline (such as that displayed in Timeline figure, see earlier in this chapter). This can help the student memorise information within a sequence – an aspect that is challenging for students with dyslexia.

Contributing to a discussion exercise, or a group presentation, can have positive consequences for the dyslexic learner's self-esteem. Working in groups can also provide the learner with practice at experimenting and becoming more familiar with his/her own learning style. It is important, according to Dargie, that students with dyslexia gain experience in the range of specific skills needed for history such as the ability to question, infer, deduce, propose, estimate, guess, judge and to think.

Learning to talk about history can provide a launch pad for reading and writing about history. Similarly, paired homework, with an emphasis upon pupils having to check that their partner can readily explain topic vocabulary, can also provide the confidence to write. It is important to plan and anticipate the types of difficulties the student with dyslexia may experience in history. One example of this can be listening skills. Listening skills can be enhanced by providing dyslexic pupils with topic content in audio cassette form for individual use in Walkman-type players. Many excellent audio resources exist for most history courses, particularly those broadcast by the BBC. Although there are difficulties in listening to audio programmes the practice can be beneficial, and they can be valuable in helping individual learners rehearse topic vocabulary before a lesson, or for reinforcement purposes.

According to Dargie (2001), it is also important that history departments plan a reading strategy that seeks to create 'more self-aware' readers who understand the purpose of their reading and who appreciate how and why the text in front of them is shaped in the way that it is. An effective reading strategy in history might include features such as:

- consistent teacher pre-checking of text material and calculation of reading age to ensure pupils encounter historical text in a planned, progressive way;
- a focus upon concept vocabulary and upon discursive connectives which develop historical argument;
- the selective use of wordprocessing functions such as emboldening and/or increasing point size to highlight the way historical text works;
- the planned reading of material as homework to increase pupil familiarity with the demands of the text using scissors and highlighter pens to analyse how different kinds of historical text are constructed;
- highlighting photocopied text to given criteria e.g. in search of key phrases;
- persistent teacher questioning to accompany pupil reading to check comprehension. This is particularly important when working with dyslexic readers who may only have partially automatised the decoding of print, and who may not yet be self-generating questions as they read;
- teacher awareness of the different preferred reading styles of pupils, and of the interactive nature of effective reading;
- teacher awareness of the difficulties posed by 'weasel words' in history such as class, state, party, church which have an abstract historical usage in addition to their more familiar common concrete meaning;
- teacher alertness to the difficulties posed by subject specific conventions such 'c.' for 'circa', 'IV' for 'fourth', 'C.' for 'century' etc.;
- teacher awareness of the need to structure their own text to meet the needs of different learners e.g. by avoiding long, multi-clausal sentences, avoiding over use of passive voice constructions, planning in ways of explaining unfamiliar vocabulary and ideas e.g. word boxes and marginal scaffolding, keeping text concrete where appropriate rather than abstract, minimising the use of metaphorical language, being alert to the range of tenses used in history to describe actions in the past. (Dargie, 2001, p. 76)

Examinations can cause considerable anxiety for students with dyslexia and these can be dealt with by the history department through recognition of the kind of exam anxiety dyslexic students can experience. It is also useful to provide specific study skills aimed at examination revision and ensuring that the student revises effectively and uses the time available efficiently. It is often the case that students with dyslexia spend a considerable length of time revising, but often to no avail – it is important then that such effort that is generated by the student is rewarded. Guidance and support in study and study techniques, therefore, is as crucial as the students' knowledge and understanding of the actual content of the subject.

Physics

Physics is a subject that can present some difficulties to dyslexic students, but it is also one of the subjects in which they can do well because it may involve less reading and a high degree of scientific understanding. Holmes (2001) suggests a top-down approach, first providing a whole-school awareness of dyslexia and allowing subject teachers to reflect on the implications of providing for dyslexic students in their own subject. Other factors which Holmes considers include:

* building a bank of support materials that can become a whole-school resource;
* recognising the implications of secondary difficulties which can affect a students performance in a particular subject – for example, the relationship between mathematics and physics that can mean that the student's difficulties in physics are a consequence of mathematics difficulties.

These emphasise the need for a whole-school approach on dealing with dyslexia.

Drama

Drama is also a subject that should be enjoyable and easily accessed by students with dyslexia – often, however, it is not. There is much more to drama than reading plays and it is important that the dyslexic person becomes actively involved in all aspects of drama.

This can include planning the sets and designing costumes. Gray (2001) suggests that students can perhaps work in pairs through the various scenes in a play, complete columns with lists of props, character costumes, and ideas for scenery. Eadon (2005) suggests that many ideas can come from the students themselves and it is important to allow students to take some initiative, especially since students with dyslexia can have some very innovative ideas. This of course can also help to boost self-esteem.

It is usually very useful to present scripts in a larger than normal type size. It is also helpful to use a dyslexia-friendly type face, such as Comic Sans, Times New Roman or the Sassoon fonts. The script should also be spaced out to make it easier to read – in fact each sentence can be on a new line.

One of the important aspects about drama is that it has cross-curricular implications. Drama can have a positive spin-off effect in English, art and other subjects. Subjects such as drama have the opportunity to boost a student's self-concept and this can have a transferable effect to other subject areas. (For details see Eadon, 2005).

Implications for other subjects

These examples above highlight how different subject areas can be accessed for dyslexic children. They also illustrate that the suggestions, and the principles upon which these suggestions are based, can be applied across the whole curriculum. All subjects, including the sciences and the social sciences and subjects of a more practical and technical orientation can be made dyslexia-friendly. The key principles include planning as well as an awareness of dyslexia and the difficulties and the strengths shown by students with dyslexia. It is also important to recognise the role of learning styles and the need to present information in a manner and mode that is consistent with the learner's learning style. One cannot underestimate the potential of cross-curricular learning and the importance of this for students with dyslexia. Of great importance is the development of self-esteem – this usually comes from success and it is crucial that the student with dyslexia experiences success in at least some of the subject areas. But all subject teachers can make accommodations to meet the needs of dyslexic students and clearly planning and differentiation are essential to achieve this.

Differentiation

Differentiation has been described as 'the action necessary to respond to the individual's requirements for curriculum access.' (DfEE and QCA, 1999)

Essentially therefore, the differentiation required for dyslexic students should not be seen as a 'special case', but an essential component of preparation which would be carried out for all pupils. Williams and Lewis (2001) in relation to geography recognise that differentiation can take place:

- *by task* – i.e. providing the student with a range of tasks from which to select;
- *by outcome* – which means using a range of assessment strategies in order that the dyslexic student can demonstrate their knowledge and understanding of the subject;
- *by support* – essentially this can include support staff but also parents, school management and collaboration.

It is suggested that differentiation does not mean writing worksheets with reduced content. Factors such as these shown below can be useful:

- knowledge of the readability levels of text and sources of information;
- the design of resources, including the layout and the use of diagrams, the latter needs to be clearly labelled;
- provision of printed materials such as notes and maps to prevent tracing and arduous note taking;
- the provision of key words – this is important as this can help to provide the student with a framework of the topic and prevent any difficulties he/she may display with word retrieval;
- specialised vocabulary spelling lists, this is important as in some science subjects there may be a specialised technical vocabulary;
- tape recordings of key passages can also be helpful as these can obviously be replayed by the student. It needs to be remembered, however, that there can be time implications with this so it should be adopted prudently.

Key issues

Some of the key issues relating to dyslexia in the secondary school include:

- the subject content – ensuring it is accessible;
- subject delivery – ensuring that the presentation of the curriculum acknowledges the learning style and the strengths of students with dyslexia and that the planning takes into account the potential difficulties they may experience with the subject;
- assessment – as far as possible a wide range of assessment strategies should be used;
- cross-curricular aspects – it is important that opportunities for collaboration with other subject teachers are provided as this can promote any cross-curricular transfer of knowledge and any particular concepts that can apply across different subject areas are noted;
- learning styles – it is important to acknowledge the fact that new learning needs to be presented in a manner that can suit the student's learning style;
- training for staff in the area of dyslexia is important as all staff should have at least an awareness of dyslexia.

It is important, therefore, that these issues are fully addressed in order that the student with dyslexic difficulties can achieve some success in different subject areas. Teaching and learning should be planned together. This implies that knowledge of teaching strategies and of the learner's individual strengths, difficulties and learning style are all necessary in order for planning and presentation of learning to be effective.

Hunter (2001), in referring to the layout of the science classroom, highlights potential pitfalls relating particularly to organisation of group work that can result in the dyslexic student missing vital information if, for example, the student is seated out of view of demonstrations or even the board. There are organisational implications here particularly if there are booklets and materials to refer to which need to be readily accessible and readily identifiable. The laboratory setting can, however, be very compatible with the learning style of a dyslexic student as it provides scope and space for group work, and flexibility in approaches to learning.

Other subjects such as modern foreign languages, art and design and design and technology which can prove challenging in terms of the amount of reading can lend themselves quite easily to kinaesthetic approaches by focusing on experiential learning activities.

For example, modern foreign languages are often seen as a source of considerable difficulty for the dyslexic student and consequently frustration for the teacher. Crombie and McColl (2001) show that by using appropriate strategies and considering the mode of presentation, dyslexic students can achieve success.

For example they suggest the following:

- the use of charts and diagrams to highlight the bigger picture;
- adding mime and gesture to words;
- adding pictures to text;
- using colour to highlight gender, accents;
- labelling diagrams and charts;
- using games to consolidate vocabulary;
- making packs of pocket size cards;
- using different colours for different purposes;
- combining listening and reading by providing text and tape;
- using mind maps, spidergrams;
- allowing student to produce their own tape;
- presenting information in small amounts, using a variety of means, with frequent opportunities for repetition and revision; and
- providing an interest in the country, through showing films, and highlighting literature and culture.

Generally it is important in most subjects for instructions to be short and clear, preferably using bullet points. It is also worth considering the use of labels and key terms to highlight various points – the dyslexic student often has a word-finding difficulty and may need for some of the terms used in some subject areas to be reinforced.

Other considerations

Thinking skills

It is important to consider the development of higher order thinking skills when teaching children with dyslexia. There may be a tendency to overlook these types of programmes in preference for a more direct decoding/literacy acquisition type of intervention. Some forms of assessment, such as dynamic assessment discussed in Chapter 1, which involves providing the learner with assistance during the assessment process, offer an opportunity to utilise thinking skills. This form of assessment encourages the learner to articulate the thinking process, e.g. why he/she thinks a certain response is correct. This approach essentially links assessment and teaching and highlights the child's learning process.

Multilingualism

Usmani (1999) suggests the bilingual, bicultural child may have a broad range of thinking skills which may go undetected if the professional is unaware of the cultural values or fails to understand them in relation to the assessment and teaching programme.

Bilingualism/multilingualism is an area that can present a challenge to those involved in assessment and teaching of learners with dyslexia. Although considerable progress has been made in the development of teacher-friendly assessment and teaching materials for dyslexia, it has been assumed that these materials would be suitable for all children with dyslexic difficulties, irrespective of their cultural and social background. This may not be the case.

The British Psychological Working Party Report (BPS, 1999) emphasises the importance of culturally relevant materials for children with dyslexia and particularly culture-fair assessment. Dyslexia, the report suggests, may be 'masked by limited mastery of the language of tuition' (p.60). It is acknowledged in the report that dyslexia can occur across languages, cultures, socio-economic status, race and gender. Yet the report notes that the tools needed to uncover the masking of dyslexic difficulties are not readily available. Furthermore the message which this gives to teachers is that the key reason why a child is not acquiring literacy skills in the language being taught is the bilingual dimension, and not due to any other factor such as dyslexia.

Many of the teaching approaches suggested for bilingual children are essentially an adaptation of those suggested in Chapter 2, which are aimed mainly at monolingual dyslexic learners. It is important that this adaptation occurs following consultation with school staff, support staff and specialist teachers and are contextualised for the bilingual child. However, as Deponio, Landon and Reid (2000) indicate, care should be taken to note that some bilingual learners may have difficulty articulating some sounds, especially English vowels and final consonantal morphemes, and speakers of syllable-timed languages such as Cantonese, may have difficulty in hearing unstressed syllables in stress-timed English utterances. Previous experience of reading logographic, as opposed to alphabetic, script may also cause difficulties with analogical reading for a literate Chinese pupil. Therefore, more practice in recognising rhyme and syllable may be necessary for learners from certain language backgrounds.

The use of computers and technology

Materials for learners with dyslexia can be enriched through the use of computer programs. There are a number of companies that specialise in software for learners with dyslexia. One such company is iANSYST Ltd. (website: www.dyslexic.com). They provide a full range of text to speech software using the more advanced RealSpeak® voices which are a significant improvement on previous versions with a much more human sounding voice. Such software can be very helpful for proofreading as it is easier to hear mistakes than to see them and it can help to identify if any words arc in the wrong place. iANSYST recommend software such as Wordsmith V2 as it can scan and edit paper-based text and images, listen to text being read back and can help the learner explore creative writing with speech support. The TextHelp® range is also highly recommended. TextHelp Type and Touch 4.0 has integrated speech output for PC or Apple Mac and includes the text help spellchecker which has been specifically developed for use by learners with dyslexia. Other computer support includes the Quicktionary Reading Pen that transfers words from the page to the LCD display when scanned by the pen. The package can be upgraded to extend its capabilities in order to convert it into a translator with over 20 different languages available. The reading pen also speaks the words and can define the word when requested. There are also a number of typing tuition programs that can assist with the development of touch-typing. These include the KAZ Typing Tutor which has an age range of seven to adult and First Keys to Literacy which has a recommended age range of 5–9 years. Some of the keyboarding activities include word lists, individual letter recognition, digraphs and rhymes, and picture, letter and word prompts. There is also a program called Magictype which is a fun, interactive programme for the 6–11 age range.

There is also a wide range of software on study skills and memory training. Two such programs developed by Jane Mitchell include Mastering Memory and Time 2 Revise/Timely Reminders. Mastering Memory helps to improve short-term memory, enhances the learner's capacity to transfer new information to other areas of learning and enhances long-term retention.

Time 2 Revise/Timely Reminders are packages that can help to structure the revision process and utilise mind maps, index cards, and revision notes. The emphasis is on encouraging the student to use the facts rather than rote learning of them. This active learning has been shown to be significantly more successful in retention and recall as well as enhancing understanding. There are also other popular programs that help to organise information such as Kidspiration for the 5–11 age range and Inspiration, which is also suitable for adults. These help to develop ideas and concepts with examples of concept maps and templates that incorporate a range of subject areas such as languages, arts, science and social studies.

R-E-M software also produce computer materials specifically for dyslexia and have produced a catalogue in association with the BDA (website www.r-e-m.co.uk).

Dimitriadi (2000) suggests that computer technology can facilitate access to the curriculum for bilingual children. She suggests that equipment and programs can support simultaneous input from different languages in oral, written or visual format and provide bilingual learners with the opportunity to enrich the curriculum with their diverse cultural experiences. She suggests that technology can help to reinforce alphabet skills by establishing correspondence between phonemes and graphemes in one language; and making the necessary connections between the way in which apparently similar graphemes have different sounds in other languages. A talking wordprocessor provides the learners with immediate aural feedback through typing of individual graphemes.

She suggests that a voice recognition system programmed to understand regional accents and problematic utterance, will encourage the input of speech and translate it into script. This can help with spelling, allow the opportunity to self-check and to construct simple sentences. Spellcheckers with phonically constructed wordbanks facilitate the writing process by generating lists of possible alternatives. It is possible, therefore, according to Dimitriadi to include simultaneously an oral and written translation of the word rule into another language. Talking wordprocessors with pre-recorded word banks can provide immediate aural feedback to the users by repeating each word or sentence typed and the learner is prompted to self-correct the sentence they typed by seeing their spelling mistakes in the form of highlighted words.

Dimitriadi suggests that computers can help with some of the difficulties related to the directional flow of the learner's written language structure such as in Cantonese, Chinese or in Arabic scripts where the characters follow a different course to that of European languages. She suggests a multimedia computer allows learners to record their voices instead of typing the information and temporarily they overcome the burden a new script might pose.

Awareness raising

The key to successful planning and presentation of the curriculum and differentiation for dyslexic children is that all staff have an understanding of the characteristics of dyslexia and the processing style of the individual dyslexic children in their class. This can be done through awareness-raising staff training that can be directed to all staff and not a few specialists, which has been the case in many schools. Below is a list of the potential topics that can be included in awareness-raising staff development.

Topics

- What is dyslexia?
- Identification and assessment of dyslexia in the classroom
- Teaching programmes
- Teaching strategies
- Learning skills and learning styles
- Differentiation
- Using a reading scheme effectively with dyslexic children
- Planning and presenting curricular materials
- Thinking skills and the implications of this for dyslexic children
- Role of parents
- Whole-school programmes
- Study skills
- Role of computers

It can be seen from the list above that awareness-raising training can, and should, be more than a one-off snapshot and should include a carefully constructed and contextualised course over a period of time. This can pay dividends as it is very likely that every teacher in the country will have at least one child with dyslexia in his/her class.

Summary

This chapter has suggested that there is no 'off-the-shelf' answer to dealing with dyslexia. Ideally a curriculum perspective should be adopted and this implies that the onus is not on the learner but on the teacher to ensure that the curriculum and the tasks are suitably planned, presented and differentiated for children with dyslexia. Part of this involves knowledge of the child and his/her individual learning and processing style. A comprehensive and curriculum-contextualised assessment, therefore, is necessary before planning commences. It is suggested throughout this book that contextualised assessment can be conducted by the class teacher, with support from specialists if available. The class teacher will acquire knowledge of the child in the normal course of teaching the class and this knowledge is essential in the planning and presentation of the curriculum for children with dyslexia.

Chapter 4

Dyslexia and Inclusion

Inclusion

The term inclusion implies that the needs of all children should be met within the mainstream school. This seems a tall order, particularly since virtually all education authorities in the country have some form of specialised provision for children with specific needs, and many also utilise specialised provision from the independent sector. In order for children with specific difficulties to have their needs fully met in mainstream school there is a need for all teachers to be at least familiar with a range of special educational needs, including specific learning difficulties, such as dyslexia. It is suggested here that the responsibility for meeting the needs of children with dyslexia should no longer be solely vested in specialists. Certainly those teachers who have specialist training and experience can play a vitally important role. They can pass on their skills to class teachers and help to ensure that all staff have an awareness and some training in areas such as dyslexia.

Class teachers, of course, are under considerable pressure. Continuous assessment, the development of IEPs and curriculum planning can exert considerable time pressures on teachers. Some dyslexic children also require a degree of individual support and this can put added pressure onto teachers. It is possible for classroom teachers to utilise the resources and the help of others in the school to ensure the needs of dyslexic children are met. For example, a sound working knowledge of technology, support materials and how these can be used will be of enormous benefit when it comes to utilising all the support available, and in many classrooms teaching assistants are available. There are also many studies showing the advantages and the potential of using parent helpers and in working co-operatively with the home as well as using senior pupils with younger students in peer tutoring programmes (Topping, 2002).

This implies that inclusion should be seen in its broadest sense, utilising the support of community resources as well as collaboration with parents. Full inclusion can only become a reality if the whole community is included. This implies that links with community facilities such as libraries, community centres and organisations such as housing associations and co-operatives, that may not be directly involved in education, are essential, as inclusion is not only about full access to education but about social fairness and equitable distribution of resources.

At the school level this requires curriculum planning and shared objectives between home and school. Consultation and planning appear to be two of the key factors that can bring about such equity and consequently full access to the curriculum. These will be discussed later in this chapter.

Inclusion – meeting needs

In 2001, a revised Code of Practice for England and Wales was issued by the Secretary of State for Education, giving guidance to education authorities on their duties in making special provision for pupils. This means that legally, local authorities must have regard to the provisions of the Code, therefore education authorities need to uphold the fundamental principles of the Code – entitlement to a broad curriculum, integration, pupil self-advocacy and parental involvement.

The importance of the Code of Practice in England and Wales, however, is that it is enforceable by law. This means that education authorities must meet the child's educational needs and that the provision identified in the statement is actually implemented.

In Scotland the approximate equivalent to a statement is the Record of Needs, although this is currently the subject of significant revision and reform. The expected legislative replacement for the Record of Needs is contained in the consultative document 'Additional Support for Learning' (Scottish Executive, 2003). This document introduces a new duty on education authorities to identify and address the additional support needs of pupils and the document suggests this goes much wider than the current special educational needs framework. Additional support needs in this context means 'needs for support that are additional to those which other children normally receive, in order to help a child benefit from education and so make the educational progress which is expected of him/her'. The document suggests that education authorities will not have to assess every child formally to establish whether they have any additional support needs, but they will be expected to take steps to ensure that the reasons for a child's lack of progress are identified and appropriate action is taken. Formal assessment, therefore, is only one means that can help identify the support needs of that individual child. This has implications for children with dyslexia and clearly places more responsibility on the teacher to identify and assess the needs of children with dyslexia. Although this can be challenging for many, especially since awareness of dyslexia is still relatively low in some areas, it can help teachers adopt an approach where the key aspect is identification of the 'barriers to learning'.

Essentially, with developed and appropriately funded school and authority policies on dyslexia there should be no need to rely on the Record of Needs procedures. Scotland has opted heavily towards a model of early intervention. A number of well-funded projects throughout Scotland have been implemented and these have attempted to ensure that the needs of children with dyslexia are identified early. This, together with the high priority on special educational needs training (Mackay and McLarty, 1999), the flexibility of the 5–14 curriculum (Crombie and Reid, 1994), and the impetus for early identification as a result of the early intervention programme, can mean that the structures and the practices are in place. Nevertheless local variation in the satisfaction of parents of children with dyslexia is still evident (Reilly, Personal Communication, 2003).

These legislative and government driven initiatives should pave the way for the development of the practices that can lead to an inclusive school. Much of the success of this in relation to dyslexia, however, rests on the need for effective communication between parents and school in relation to shared concerns and attitudes over the most appropriate provision and curriculum for children with dyslexia.

Principles and practices of inclusion

Assessment, need and accountability

One of the key features of educational provision in most countries involves the concept of accountability. Governments demand results, schools want results and parents expect results. How these 'results' are measured is a matter of debate. The government's expectations may be measured differently by schools and by parents – the measure of progress can be dependent on how one views the purpose of education and the means of achieving that purpose. These two variables 'purpose' and 'means' may differ, even within an inclusive setting. Inclusion, therefore, is not the educational product but the educational vehicle that can contain the methods, means and purposes of the educational experience for all students. That experience, however, can be dependent on, and even restricted by, the need for accountability, as it attempts to define the educational experience into a measurable commodity. National testing, government benchmarks and league tables to identify 'high performing' and 'low performing' schools are examples of political pressures on an education system. These seek to serve 'all', but recognise that the individual differences in children mean that 'all' will not progress in the same way, and at the same rate. An enlightened education system would not expect that, but the reality of market forces and accountability of the public purse may determine the nature of the educational process in schools and the educational experience of children in the classrooms. Some groups of learners may be a casualty of this drive to measure achievement. Viall (2000) argues, for example, that this practice of 'high stakes assessment' in the United States which is intended to measure and enhance student progress can in fact be discriminatory in relation to students with dyslexia.

These 'high stakes' tests are usually standardised, as is also the case in the UK with national testing, and many of these types of tests do not make accommodation for the needs of dyslexic students, nor in fact for the needs of students from different cultures. Moreover, Viall argues that this practice carries a risk of the teacher teaching to the tests and neglecting the importance of critical thinking and the metacognitive aspects of learning. One of Viall's suggestions to overcome this potentially discriminatory practice is that there should be meaningful alternative assessment which takes into account the type of difficulties experienced by students with dyslexia. This is different from providing support or examination allowances in conventional examination systems to aid the student with dyslexia – alternative assessment means 'different' assessment. This would need a complete re-think of the aims and objectives of the examination system and the need to identify exactly what are the important elements to assess, and how that assessment could be performed in an equitable fashion. There has been some evidence of this in examples of portfolio assessment that have the potential to examine the performances of students with dyslexia in a much fairer way than a one-off test or national examination.

The challenge

Inclusion is a term that has a universal currency. The term can be associated with equality, fairness and the individual's right to a democratic share of the country's resources – political, educational, economic and social. These aspects are not free-standing – each relate and interact with the other.

The challenge facing educators today in relation to inclusion results from conflicts arising from traditional pedagogical perspectives, social attitudes, conventions and perceptions. The remainder of this chapter will, therefore, examine some of these challenges and conflicts, particularly within the context of meeting the needs of children with dyslexia. These challenges are encapsulated in the five signposts for inclusion shown below. These signposts summarise many of the points made throughout this book.

Five signposts to inclusion

Signpost 1 ⟶ **Acknowledging differences**

While it is accepted that there are common factors in dyslexia, (BPS, 1999; Report of the Task Force on Dyslexia, Republic of Ireland, 2001; Reid, 2003), it is essential that these do not dictate pedagogical approaches and that the individual differences of children with dyslexia are acknowledged. It is more helpful therefore, rather than ask the question, 'What is the best approach for dyslexic children?', to ask 'What are the barriers that prevent that child from learning?' (Wearmouth, Soler and Reid, 2002). This implies that the needs of each child should be viewed within the learning situation, and environmental and curricular factors should also be considered alongside any cognitive aspects that may impinge on learning. Morton and Frith (1995), Frith (2002) provide a framework, the causal modelling framework, that can be used to help identify these barriers. The framework consists of biological, cognitive, behavioural and environmental factors and emphasises the interactive nature of learning. The framework also emphasises the different profiles that can be associated with dyslexia. Indeed in the UK the BPS working party report on dyslexia (BPS, 1999) identified ten different hypotheses that can relate to dyslexia. Additionally the Task Force Report (Government of Ireland, 2002) indicated that 'since the difficulties presented by students with dyslexia range along a continuum from mild to severe, there is a need for a continuum of interventions and other services' (p. 31).

Therefore, it is crucial that the identification and planning for intervention for children with dyslexia acknowledges this continuum and the individual differences associated with this as well as the role of classroom and environmental factors.

Signpost 2 ⟶ **Recognising strengths**

There has been considerable pressure from many groups and individuals (Johnson and Peer, 2003; Sayles, 2001; Reid, 2003; West, 1997) to recognise the strengths of children with dyslexia. If the barriers to literacy can be removed or minimised these strengths can be revealed, and the child will be able to access the curriculum and fulfil his/her potential. It is important, therefore, to ensure that literacy, however important, does not impede progress in learning and thinking.

Multiple intelligences approaches (Garner, 1999; Lazear, 1999) highlighting eight ways of learning and, of course, effective differentiation in terms of presentation of material, can both be used as a pathway to effective learning.

The multiple intelligences framework can have particular applicability for students with dyslexia. Lazear (1999) highlights how these can be used, not only in individual subjects, but across the whole curriculum to ensure metacognitive transfer. One example of this can be the use of visual imagery combined with music – practice at this can help the student develop visual abilities and if he/she were to verbalise these it can have a spin-off effect on language and storytelling. He also indicates how the reverse can apply when students can try to impose appropriate sound into a story they have read. Similarly bodily/kinaesthetic intelligence can be applied in all subjects – in history a dramatic account of a historical incident can help develop bodily/kinaesthetic intelligence, as can learning particular folk dances from different cultures and different historical periods. Bodily/kinaesthetic intelligence is one that is often overlooked in class subjects and this, and some of the other 'intelligences' in the multiple intelligences model, can highlight the strengths of young people with dyslexia.

The work of Galaburda (1993), and the examples from West (1997) and Reid (2003) highlight the potential creativity and problem-solving skills of children and adults with dyslexia.

Signpost 3 ⟶ **Understanding inclusion**

Wearmouth, Soler and Reid (2002) suggest that the current educational context is one that attempts to reconcile the principles of individuality, distinctiveness and diversity with inclusion and equal opportunities. This, however, can highlight inherent conflicts, tensions and contradictions. There is a drive to raise the learning and achievement standards of all pupils through whole-class and whole-group teaching, standardised assessment and the encouragement of competition between schools through a focus on league tables based on academic performance. Yet at the same time there is a statutory obligation to acknowledge the principle of inclusion for all pupils, including those with significant difficulties in the development of literacy skills such as children with dyslexia. One of the key dilemmas in understanding inclusion is the reconciliation of the challenges of diversity with the need to provide common curricular objectives and a whole-class pedagogy for all. It is important, therefore, to develop inclusive models of support that can take into account the individual needs of children with dyslexia. These may not always be met, for all children, all of the time, within mainstream education, but for most they can. It is realistic to appreciate that not all children will benefit from mainstream provision without some preparation on the part of the child and the teacher. This point is made by Johnson (2001) when he quotes an extract from the DfEE guidance on inclusion:

> For most children (with special educational needs) placement in a mainstream school leads naturally on to other forms of inclusion. For those with more complex needs, the starting point should always be the question, 'Could this child benefit from education in a

mainstream setting?' For some children a mainstream placement
may not be right, or not right just yet. (DfEEa 1998, p. 23)

This implies that full inclusion in a mainstream setting for some groups
of children, although socially desirable, may not be educationally
appropriate at a given point in time. This means that, with support, all
children can aspire towards an inclusive educational environment, but
there should not be an assumption that for all this is the best practice at
every point in their school career. There are examples in practice of
children with dyslexia, who have initially failed in an inclusive setting,
but after a period of supportive and appropriate teaching in a structured
and dedicated resource for dyslexia, are able to return to a mainstream
setting and benefit more effectively, socially and educationally, from
mainstream school (Lannen, 2003; Calder, 2001).

Lannen cites the experience at the Red Rose School, a dedicated short-
term provision for children with specific learning difficulties in Lancashire,
England. Most of the children admitted to the school have failed in the
mainstream setting and have, not surprisingly, low levels of self-esteem, as
well as low attainments. But within this specialised resource the children
progress and all are eventually re-admitted to mainstream schools or
further education. Even within this dedicated special provision it can be
argued that the principles of inclusion are operating. All children within
this environment have an entitlement to the full curriculum and to have
their social, emotional and educational needs met. Inclusion needs to be
seen as a flexible package to meet the diverse needs of children.
Mainstream schools can be part of that package, but just because a child
with dyslexia is sitting in a mainstream classroom does not mean that child
is receiving the benefits of an inclusive education.

Calder (2001) describes an example of a specialised resource base in
Scotland that attempts to respect the students' needs to be part of an
inclusive educational environment. This resource is essentially a
'customised package' which aims to help students access the 'common'
curriculum. Because the package is customised to their specific needs it
is possible for the students to achieve educationally. Again these children
need to receive individual support and individual consideration before
their needs can be met in this setting.

This type of provision relies on comprehensive assessment, full
multi-professional and parental involvement, appropriate differentiation
as well as the building of self-esteem, the encouragement of learner
autonomy and the development of necessary skills for learning and for
life. According to Calder this formula is based on 'an eclectic mix of
strategies and approaches; pragmatism; customisation of the balance of
the child's needs and his/her preferences and the reconciliation of a well-
established collaborative approach with some specialised interventions
to suit the students' needs'. It is clear that the example cited by Calder

is the product of considerable planning and preparation – this, including the training of staff, is essential.

Inclusion, therefore, should be seen as a comprehensive package specifically tailored for the individual to ensure the social and educational benefits are maximised for all. This package is recognised in the Republic of Ireland Task Force Report when it recommends that

> special schools for students with specific learning difficulties, including dyslexia, should be developed as resource centres for special class teachers and resource teachers working with students with learning difficulties arising from dyslexia, through the development of links with local education centres. (p. 113)

This highlights the need for an inclusive package to be flexible to take account of children's needs and local variations and preferences.

Signpost 4 ⟶ Planning for practice

The learning environment is one of the most influential factors in relation to planning intervention. It is important to engage in multi-disciplinary assessment and collaboration to plan programmes which should be embedded into the whole-school curriculum. Wearmouth (2001) argues that the complexity of the issues relating to inclusion must be tackled and policy-makers need to understand the long-term nature of embedding change of this nature in relation to the teacher development and the provision of resources and technology. On the one hand, therefore, while inclusion can be seen as a desirable outcome in terms of equity, it can also be seen as a threat and a potential conflict between meeting the needs of individuals within a framework that has to be established to meet the needs of all.

Differentiation and curricular development are both challenges and indeed responses to meeting the needs of students with dyslexia. It is important that the learning experiences of children with dyslexia are contextualised and meaningful. Differentiation can help to make subject content meaningful and curriculum development such as developing thematic units of work can make curriculum content cohesive and meaningful.

Kirk (2001) suggests that it is important that the common features which most subjects share can be utilised to help the student develop concepts and automaticity. For example, she argues, all subjects foster the capacity to think, to communicate, to solve problems, to engage with others, and to acquire important skills of various kinds, and that failure to recognise these features can lead to a limitation of the educational experiences for students with dyslexia.

There are many examples of differentiation that have been the product of consultative collaboration within school departments (Lucas,

2002; personal communication, Dodds, 1996). Ideally the needs of students with dyslexia should be met in this way and the resources and guidance on differentiation can provide a framework for the development of a differentiated approach. One of the important points to consider is that, although the language and sentence structure may be different and the overall plan of the page designed in a user-friendly fashion in a differentiated text, the underlying concepts that are to be taught should be the same. Therefore, the cognitive demands and the learning outcomes should be the same for all learners – differentiation, therefore, means that the routes or modes of learning to achieve these outcomes will be different, but not the conceptual outcomes.

Wearmouth and Reid (2002) report on the influence of Bronfenbrenner's model. They indicate how the learning environment can produce barriers to pupils' learning and that the ecosystemic perspective developed by Bronfenbrenner (1979) is useful because it identifies four levels that influence child outcomes: the microsystem, the immediate context of the child – school, classrooms, home, neighbourhood; the mesosystem, the links between two microsystems, e.g. home–school relationships; the exosystem, outside demands/influences in adults' lives that affect children; and macrosystem, cultural beliefs/patterns or institutional policies that affect individuals' behaviour.

This indicates the importance of multi-disciplinary collaboration and in particular between the various organisations and agencies at an administrative level as well as those professionals who represent them. Examples of this can be noted in a number of government initiatives in England, Wales, Scotland and Ireland. One example of this can also be noted in the Task Force Report (Government of Ireland, 2001) the recommendation, as a medium-term goal, of the establishment of an inter-departmental committee that includes 'representatives of the Departments of Enterprise and Employment; Health and Children; Social, Community and Family Affairs; Justice, Equality and Law Reform; and Finance to ensure the needs of students with learning difficulties arising from dyslexia are addressed in a co-ordinated manner' (p. 112).

Signpost 5 ⟶ Attainable outcomes

There is a current trend, perhaps an obsession, with measuring educational 'progress'. This means that greater importance is placed on these variables that can be easily measured. That is not to say that such assessments cannot help to inform practice (Shiel, 2002). But it can be argued that traditional forms of assessment can disadvantage the dyslexic student because usually there is a discrepancy, and this may be a significant discrepancy, between their understanding of a topic and how they are able to display that understanding in written form.

There is evidence that portfolio assessment, which has the potential to exam the performances of students with dyslexia in a much fairer way than a one-off test or national examinations, should have a greater impact on the examination system.

It can be argued that any deficit or difficulty may not lie with the student with dyslexia, but with an assessment process that is unable to accommodate for the diversity of learners. It can be advocated, therefore, that both teaching and assessment should be differentiated and diversified.

It is also important that learning outcomes should be clearly specified and attainable. For students with dyslexia this may mean some reference to additional support or examination accommodations, but the key aspect to attainable outcomes lies as much at the heart of curriculum development as it does in the assessment process.

Key factors

Some of the key factors in relation to successful inclusion and, in particular, children with dyslexia, include:

- a commitment by the education authority and the school to an inclusive ideal;
- a realisation by staff of the widely embracing features of inclusion and the equity issues inherent in these features;
- awareness of the particular specific needs associated with children with dyslexia and accommodation for these through curriculum and teaching approaches;
- acceptance that inclusion is more than integration and that it embraces social, cultural and community issues as well as educational equality;
- regard for the cultural differences in communities and families and acknowledgement that children with dyslexia require flexible approaches in assessment and teaching; and
- honouring not only the child's individual rights, but the individual differences.

Comment

The five signposts to inclusion for children with dyslexia – acknowledging the differences, recognising strengths, understanding inclusion, planning for practice and attainable outcomes, highlight the challenges and the needs of children with dyslexia if full and effective inclusion is to be a reality. It is recognised that one of the most crucial elements in effective learning is self-esteem. In the wrong setting and learning environment, using inappropriate curricular and learning materials, self-esteem can be adversely affected. It is important, therefore, that while inclusion is desirable for all children, including children with dyslexia, that flexibility prevails and that the individual needs of children are acknowledged.

Conclusion

This book suggests that dyslexia should not be viewed from a narrow perspective, but from one that is multi-faceted. For that reason it is important that teachers have a full understanding of the different dimensions that can contribute to dyslexia. The model discussed briefly in Chapter 1 of this book – the causal modelling framework – recognises that dyslexia can be understood from the neurological, cognitive, educational/classroom perspectives and it is helpful to recognise this.

This book has suggested some strategies at the cognitive level, such as the need to develop memory skills, to make connections between existing knowledge and new information and to generally acknowledge the information processing style and difficulties experienced by children with dyslexia. While it is appreciated that dyslexic children share common difficulties and processing styles, the individual differences also need to be recognised.

The challenge is to acknowledge these differences while dealing with the everyday demands of classroom teaching. One way of doing this is through recognition of learning styles. This is one of the key themes in this book. Learning styles can help to equip the child with self-knowledge, and this can in turn lead to autonomy in learning. This is vital for children with dyslexia, as they will not always have a support teacher, or a class teacher, to assist their learning.

The other challenge is to respond to the needs of dyslexic children within a mainstream setting and within the demands of the curriculum. This can be achieved through effective differentiation, but above all, by forward planning and collaboration. Planning for learning and anticipating the aspects of the curriculum that will be difficult for dyslexic children is vital for a whole-school strategy for inclusion.

Chapter 3 of this book suggests three aspects of support – planning, presentation and materials. There is a tendency to focus on the materials suggesting that with the right resources and materials dyslexic children will be able to learn effectively. Clearly appropriate resources are vital but this does not preclude the need for the teacher to embark on curricular planning and differentiation as a means of meeting the needs of dyslexic children. It is perhaps more helpful to view the difficulties experienced by dyslexic children as barriers to learning. It follows that if these barriers can be identified through examining the curriculum and nature of the tasks presented to the child·then this will go a long way towards meeting these needs.

There is no 'off-the-shelf' ready-made answer or programme that suits all dyslexic children. It is necessary for the teacher to be flexible and versatile in the development of resources and teaching strategies. For that reason it is indicated in this book that training for class teachers in the area of dyslexia is crucial. This training does not need to be highly specialised, but should include an awareness of the difficulties associated with dyslexia, how these can be identified and how these can be overcome within the curriculum. By taking a curriculum perspective one can more readily identify the barriers to learning and identify the tasks and the aspects of the curriculum that the child with dyslexia may have difficulties with.

There are of course some well-founded principles for teaching children with dyslexia. These include multi-sensory and overlearning. Multi-sensory because children with dyslexia can have difficulty in learning through the auditory modality and therefore need visual, kinaesthetic and tactile stimuli in order for information to be processed. Overlearning is necessary in order to achieve automaticity so that learning can be consolidated. It has been shown that dyslexic children often take longer to develop automaticity, particularly if they do not use a skill or word regularly.

Regular practice in reading and using words in a multi-sensory manner in different contexts is crucial. It is also crucial that dyslexic children gain experience in the use of language. This means that top-down approaches to reading focusing on language experience, are necessary even though the child may still not have basic word attack skills. Learning to read involves a mixture of both bottom-up phonic skills and top-down language experiences. Both can help to build decoding skills and the development of concepts and ideas. Both are essential aspects of reading. There is a tendency to neglect the development of concepts and higher-order thinking skills with dyslexic children because of their difficulties in decoding. But decoding should not take priority over the development of higher-order thinking skills. Reading is not only about accessing print, but about understanding the meaning of text and transmitting cultural and conceptual understanding to the reader. This should encourage metacognitive thinking and questioning, which in turn can develop self-sufficiency in learning.

The opening chapter of this book provides explanations of dyslexia. This is necessary as there are a number of misconceptions about dyslexia fuelled by the media reports of 'miracle cures'. A full under-standing of dyslexia will help teachers evaluate the merits of innovative or alternative approaches. It is too easy to be swayed by vigorous marketing and commercial activities.

The opening chapter also provides examples of identification and assessment. Many still see this as the realm of experts, and to an extent it is, as a full psychological assessment, which is often required, is a specialised activity. But the class teacher has a key role to play as not all children will require a full and comprehensive psychological assessment. Observation, as well as knowledge of the child, is crucial in both assessment and intervention.

Chapter 2 provides the link between assessment, teaching and learning. This link is essential – assessment in isolation is not very helpful. Similarly intervention should not only be about teaching programmes and approaches. It is necessary to examine the learning process and, in particular, how that can be applied and maximised by dyslexic children. Knowledge of learning styles and the importance of the classroom environment is, therefore, as crucial as the knowledge of teaching resources.

Chapter 3 takes this one step further and emphasises the role of the teacher in planning and presenting the curriculum to ensure that children with dyslexia have full curriculum access. Differentiation with full knowledge of the curriculum, awareness of learning styles and the learning environment and a full understanding of dyslexia can go a long way to supporting and ensuring that the learning potential of dyslexic children is maximised, within the mainstream setting. The message here is that there is not necessarily an off-the-shelf answer to classroom intervention for dyslexic children. For that reason staff development on dyslexia for class teachers and school management is necessary to provide this understanding and the opportunities and the confidence to deal with the learning needs of dyslexic children in mainstream education.

Inclusion is currently a key theme in education and this presents considerable challenges to teachers, particularly those with some responsibility for children with specific difficulties. The final chapter indicates some key aspects in helping to include dyslexic children in mainstream education, but clearly each child is unique, and each offers an individual set of challenges to teachers and schools.

One of the key aspects is the acknowledgement of self-esteem and every effort should be made, irrespective of the setting, to boost the self-esteem of dyslexic children. This can be achieved through success and it is crucial that attainable goals are set in order that success can be achieved in some form. An understanding of dyslexia, knowledge of the child and of learning styles is necessary to help achieve this.

One cannot underestimate the challenge faced by teachers of ensuring the needs of dyslexic children are met in the mainstream school. It is, however, possible to deal with this effectively with support, understanding and collaboration at all levels. This should involve the school management team, parents and all aspects of practice and policy. Education policy is important and there are already many excellent examples of sound and innovative policy on dyslexia paying dividends in practice (McKay, 2001, 2004). McKay, who developed the theme of dyslexia-friendly schools, initially in Swansea, has done much to ensure that dyslexia is not seen as a within-child deficit, but as the responsibility of the school and one that needs to be shared by all. This is consistent with the theme of this book and it is hoped that teachers and management will appreciate the need for training and collaboration, in order to provide all staff with an awareness of the needs of dyslexic children, and consider the implications of this for curriculum development, the classroom environment and educational policy.

Further Information and Contacts

Website – www.gavinreid.co.uk (contains links to most of the relevant organisations in literacy and dyslexia, including government organisations) and www.redroseschool.co.uk (Red Rose School).

Better Books, 3 Paganel Drive, Dudley, DY1 4AZ. Tel: 01384 253276, Fax: 01384 253285.

Crossbow Education, 41 Sawpit Lane, Brocton, Stafford, ST17 0TE www.crossboweducation.com.

The Dyslexia Handbook; BDA, 98 London Road, Reading, RG1 5AU (published annually).

Dyslexia: A Complete Guide for Parents; Gavin Reid (2005), Wiley.

Dyslexia A Practitioners Handbook (3rd edition); Gavin Reid (2003), Wiley.

Dyslexia, An International Journal of Research and Practice; Miles T. R. (ed.) Wiley.

Dyslexia – Successful Inclusion in the Secondary School; Lindsay Peer and Gavin Reid (eds) (2001), David Fulton Publishers, London.

Dyslexia in Focus at 16 Plus – An Inclusive Teaching Approach; Jeanne Holloway (2000), NASEN Publications.

Dyslexia and Literacy – Theory and Practice; edited by Gavin Reid and Janice Wearmouth, Wiley (2002).

Get Ahead – Mind Map© Your Way to Success; Vanda North with Tony Buzan (2001), Buzan Centres, England.

Helping Children with Reading and Spelling – A Special Needs Manual; Reason, R. and Boote, R., Routledge (1994).

Helping with Reading Difficulties Key Stage 2; Jane Calver, Sandy Ranson, Dorothy Smith (1999), NASEN.

iANSYST Ltd, Fen House, 72 Fen Road, Cambridge, CB4 1UN.

Learning Works International Ltd, 9 Barrow Close, Marlborough, Wiltshire, SN8 2BD, www.learning-works.org.uk.

Listening and Literacy Index; Charles Weedon and Gavin Reid (2001), Hodder Murray, London.

Mind Genius Ygnius; Gael Ltd, SE Technology Park, East Kilbride, Scotland, G75 QOR. www.mindgenius.com, Tel: 01355 247766, helps to write mind maps and convert to different forms of text.

Phonics and Phonic Resources; Mike Hinson and Pete Smith, NASEN (1997) (still available directly from NASEN House).

Pygmalion Education Ltd, 10 Charles II Street, St James, London, SW1Y 4AA, e-mail: lkilmurry@thepygmaliongroup,com.

Reading Schemes – the NASEN guide on CD-Rom helps to locate materials using criteria such as reading level/ interest age and topics – some of the titles have sample pages available from NASEN House, 4/5 Amber Business Village, Amber Close, Amington, Tamworth, B77 4RP.

SEN Marketing Dyslexia and Special Needs Bookshop, 618 Leeds Road, Outwood, Wakefield, WF1 2LT. Tel/fax: 01924 871697 e-mail: info@sen.uk.com; www.sen.uk.com.

Special Needs Assessment Profile (SNAP); C. Weedon and G. Reid (2003), Hodder Murray, www.snapassessment.com.

Spelling and Spelling Resources; Pete Smith, Mike Hinson and Dave Smith (1998), NASEN Publications (still available directly from NASEN House).

Special Educational Needs, Inclusion and Diversity, A Textbook; Norah Frederickson and Tony Cline (2002), Open University Press, Buckingham, England.

Stass Publications – materials designed and written for speech and language therapists – 44 North Road, Ponteland, Northumberland, NE20 9UR. Fax: 01661 860440, e-mail: susan@stass.demon.co.uk.

Teachers and Parents: Together for Reading; Dorothy Smith, John Shirley, John Visser (1996), NASEN Publications (still available directly from NASEN House).

Teaching the Literacy Hour in an Inclusive Classroom: Supporting Pupils with Learning Difficulties in a Mainstream Environment; Ann Berger and Jean Gross (eds) (1999), David Fulton Publishers, London.

Working Towards Inclusive Education – Social Contexts; Peter Mittler (2000), David Fulton Publishers.

Contacts

British Dyslexia Association, 98 London Road, Reading, RG1 5AU. Helpline: 0118 966 8217, Admin: 0118 966 2677, Fax: 0118 935 1927. e-mail: helpline@bda-dyslexia.demon.co.uk or admin@bda-dyslexia.demon.co.uk. Website: http://www.bda-dyslexia.org.uk.

Dyslexia in Scotland, Unit 3, Stirling Business Centre, Wellgreen Place, Stirling, Scotland, FK8 2DZ. Tel: 01786 446 650, Fax: 01786 471 235.

Dyslexia Association of Ireland, Suffolk Chambers, 1 Suffolk Street, Dublin 2, Ireland.

Northern Ireland Dyslexia Association, 17A Newtownards Road, Belfast, BT4 3HT.

References

Arnold H. (1984) *Making Sense of It*. Hodder & Stoughton, London.

British Psychological Society (BPS) (1999) *Dyslexia, Literacy and Psychological Assessment*. British Psychological Society, Leicester.

British Psychological Society (1999) *The Directory of Chartered Psychologists*. BPS, Leicester, UK.

Bronfenbrenner, U. (1979) *The Ecology of Human Development*. Harvard University Press, Cambridge, MA.

Brown, M. (1993) 'Supporting learning through a whole-school approach' in Reid, G. (ed.), *Specific Learning Difficulties (Dyslexia) Perspectives on Practice*. Moray House Publications, Edinburgh.

Brozo, W. (2003) *Strategic Moves – role playing in thinking*, an international journal of reading, writing and critical reflection, Vol. 4 No. 2 April, pp. 43–5.

Burden, B. (2002) 'A cognitive approach to dyslexia: Learning styles and thinking skills' in G.Reid and J. Wearmouth *Dyslexia and Literacy: Theory and Practice*. Wiley.

Buzan, T. (1993) *The Mind Map Book – Radiant Thinking*. BBC Books, London.

Calder, I. (2001) 'Dyslexia across the Curriculum' in L. Peer and G. Reid (eds) *Dyslexia – Successful Inclusion in the Secondary School*. David Fulton Publishers, London.

Clay, M. (1979) *Reading: The patterning of complex behaviour*. Heinemann Educational, Auckland.

Clay, M. (1985) *The Early Detection of Reading Difficulties: A Diagnostic Survey with Recovery Procedures*. Heinemann Educational, Auckland.

Conner, M. (1994) Specific learning difficulties (dyslexia) and interventions. *Support for Learning*, 9 (3) pp. 114–19.

Cowling, H. and Cowling, K. (1998) *Toe by Toe: A Highly Structured Multisensory Reading Manual for Teachers and Parents*. Bradford, UK.

Crombie, M. and McColl, H. (2001) 'Dyslexia and the Teaching of Modern Foreign Languages' in L. Peer and G. Reid (eds), *Dyslexia – Successful Inclusion in the Secondary School*. David Fulton Publishers, London.

Crombie, M. (2002) 'Dealing with diversity in the primary classroom – a challenge for the class teacher' in G. Reid and J. Wearmouth (eds) *Dyslexia and Literacy: Theory and Practice*. Wiley.

Cudd, E. T. and Roberts, L. L. (1994) 'A scaffolding technique to develop sentence sense and vocabulary', *The Reading Teacher*, 47(4), pp. 346–9.

Dargie, R. (2001) 'Dyslexia and History' in L. Peer and G. Reid (eds) *Dyslexia – Successful Inclusion in the Secondary School*. David Fulton Publishers, London.

Deponio, Landon and Reid (2000) 'Dyslexia and Bilingualism – Implications

References

for Assessment, Teaching and Learning' in L. Peer and G. Reid (eds) *Multilingualism, Literacy and Dyslexia: A Challenge for Educators*. David Fulton Publishers, London.

DES, (1978) *Special Educational Needs* (The Warnock Report). HMSO, London.

Dodds, D. (1996) 'Differentiation in the secondary school' in G. Reid (ed.), *Dimensions of Dyslexia. Vol. 1 Assessment, Teaching and the Curriculum*. Moray House Publications, Edinburgh.

Dunn, R., Dunn, K. and Price, G. E. (1975, 1979, 1985, 1987, 1989) *Learning Styles Inventory*. Price Systems Inc, Lawrence, KA.

Department for Education and Employment (DfEE,) (1994) *The Code of Practice for the Identification and Assessment of Special Educational Needs*. DfEE, London.

Department for Education and Employment (DfEE,) (1998) *Framework for Teaching*. DfEE, London.

Department for Education and Employment (DfEE) (1996) *The National Literacy Project*. DfEE, London.

Department for Education and Employment (DfEE) (1998) *Framework for Teaching*. DfEE, London.

DfEE and QCA (1999) *The National Curriculum for England; Geography*. DfEE and QCA, London.

Department for Education and Skills (2001) *Special Educational Needs Code of Practice*. DfES, London.

Dimitriadi, Y. (2000) 'Using ICT to Support Bilingual Dyslexic Learners' in L. Peer and G. Reid (eds) *Multilingualism, Literacy and Dyslexia: A Challenge for Educators*. David Fulton Publishers, London.

Eadon, H. (2005) *Dyslexia and Drama*. David Fulton Publishers, London.

Fawcett, A. J. and Nicolson, R. I. (1996) *The Dyslexia Screening Test*. London, The Psychological Corporation, Europe.

Fawcett, A. J. and Nicolson, R. I. (2001) 'Dyslexia: The Role of the Cerebellum' in A. J. Fawcett (ed.). *Dyslexia: Theory and Good Practice*. Whurr Publications, London.

Fawcett, A. Nicolson, R. and Lee, R. (2001) *The Pre-school Screening Test (PREST)*. Psychological Corporation, Kent.

Frith, U. (2002) 'Resolving the paradoxes of dyslexia' in G. Reid and J. Wearmouth *Dyslexia and Literacy: Theory and Practice*. Wiley.

Galaburda, A. (ed.) (1993) *Dyslexia and Development: Neurobiological Aspects of Extraordinary Brains*. Harvard University Press, Cambridge, MA.

Gardner, H. (1983) *Frames of Mind*. Basic Books, New York.

Gardner, H. (1999) foreword in D. Lazear, (1999) *Eight Ways of Knowing Teaching for Multiple Intelligences*, Third edition Skylight Professional Development, Arlington Heights, Illinois, USA pp. vii–viii.

Glyn, T. and McNaughton, S. (1985) The 'managere' home and school remedial reading procedures: continuing research on their effectiveness. *New Zealand Journal of Psychology* pp. 66–77.

Goodman, K. (1976) 'Reading – a psycholinguistic guessing game' in H. Singer and R. B. Ruddell (eds), *Theoretical Models and Processes of Reading*. International Reading Association.

Gorrie, B. and Parkinson, E. (1995) *Phonological Awareness Procedure*. Stass Publications.

Gray, R. (2001) 'Drama: The experience of learning' in L. Peer and G. Reid (eds) *Dyslexia – Successful Inclusion in the Secondary School*. David Fulton Publishers, London.

Holmes, P. (2001) 'Dyslexia and Physics' in L. Peer and G. Reid (eds) *Dyslexia – Successful Inclusion in the Secondary School*. David Fulton Publishers, London.

Horne, J. K., Singleton, C. H. and Thomas, K. V. (1999) *Lucid Assessment System for Schools, Secondary Version (LASS Secondary)*. Lucid Creative Limited, Beverley, East Yorkshire.

Hunt, G. (2002) 'Critical literacy and access to the lexicon' in G. Reid and J. Wearmouth (eds) *Dyslexia and Literacy: Theory and Practice*. Wiley.

Hunter, V. (2001) 'Dyslexia and General Science' in L. Peer and G. Reid (eds) *Dyslexia – Successful Inclusion in the Secondary School*. David Fulton Publishers, London.

Johnson, M. and Peer, L. (eds) (2003) *The Dyslexia Handbook 2003*, BDA, Reading.

Johnson, M., Phillips, S. and Peer, L. (1999) *Multisensory Teaching System for Reading*, Special Educational Needs Centre, Didsbury School of Education, Manchester Metropolitan University.

Kirk, J. (2001) 'Cross-curricular approaches to staff development in secondary schools' in L. Peer and G. Reid (eds) *Dyslexia – Successful Inclusion in the Secondary School*. David Fulton Publishers, London.

Landon, J. (1999) 'Early intervention with bilingual learners: towards a research agenda' in South, H. (ed.) *Literacies in Community and School*, Watford: National Association for Language Development in the Curriculum (NALDIC), pp. 84–96.

Lannen, S. and Reid, G. (2003) 'Learning Styles: Lights, Sound, Action' in *BDA Handbook 2003*, BDA, Reading.

Lannen, S. (2003) Personal communication.

Lazear, D. (1999) *Eight Ways of Knowing: Teaching for Multiple Intelligences*, (third edition) Skylight Professional Development, Arlington Heights, Illinois, USA.

Lewis, A. and Norwich, B. (eds) (2004) *Special Teaching for Special Children? Pedagogies for Inclusion*. Open University Press, Maidenhead.

Macintyre, C. and Deponio, P. (2003) *Identifying and Supporting Children with Specific Learning Difficulties: Looking Beyond the Label to Assess the Whole Child*. Routledge/Falmer.

McKay, N. (2004) 'The Case for Dyslexia Friendly Schools' in G. Reid and A. Fawcett (eds), *Dyslexia in Context: Research, Policy and Practice*. Whurr Publications, London.

McNaughton, S. (1995) *Patterns of Emerging Literacy: Processes of Development and Transition*. Oxford University Press, Auckland.

McNaughton, S., Glynn, T. and Robinson, V. (1987) *Pause, Prompt and Praise: Effective Reading Remedial Tutoring*. Positive Products, Birmingham.

Miles, T. R. (1983) Bangor Dyslexia Test. Learning Development Aids, Cambridge.

Mittler, P. (2001) *Working Towards Inclusive Education – Social Contexts*. David Fulton Publishers, London.

Morton, J. and Frith, U. (1995) 'Causal modelling: A structural approach to developmental psychopathology' in D. Cicchetti and D. J. Cohen (eds) *Manual of Developmental Psychopathology* (pp. 357–90). NY Psychological Assessment of Dyslexia. Wiley.

Nicolson, R. I. and Fawcett, A. J. (1996) *The Dyslexia Early Screening Test*. The Psychological Corporation, London.

Nicolson, R. I, Fawcett, A. J. and Dean, P. (2001) Developmental dyslexia; The cerebella deficit hypothesis; *Trends in Neurosciences*, 24(9), pp. 508–11.

Nicolson, R. I. and Fawcett, A. J. (1990) Automaticity: a new framework for dyslexia research?; *Cognition*, p. 35, 159–82.

Nisbet, J. and Shucksmith, J. (1986) *Learning Strategies*. Routledge, London.

Northern Ireland Government (2002) *Task Group Report on Dyslexia*.

Norwich, B. and Lewis, A. (2001) Mapping a pedagogy for special educational needs. *British Educational Research Journal*, pp. 27, 3, 313–31.

Palincsar, A. and Brown, A. (1984) 'Reciprocal Teaching of Comprehension Fostering and Comprehension Monitoring Activities'. *Cognition and Instruction*, 1(2), pp. 117–75.

Peer, L. and Reid, G. (eds) (2001) *Dyslexia – Successful Inclusion in the Secondary School*. David Fulton Publishers, London.

Rack, J. (1994) 'Dyslexia: The phonological deficit hypothesis' in R. I. Nicolson and A. J. Fawcett (eds), *Dyslexia in Children: Multidisciplinary Perspectives*. Harvester Wheatsheaf, Hemel Hempstead.

Reason, R. and Boote, R. (1994) *Helping Children with Reading and Spelling: A Special Needs Manual*. Routledge, London.

Reason, R., Brown, P., Cole, M. and Gregory, M. (1988) 'Does the 'specific' in specific learning difficulties make a difference to the way we teach?' *Support for Learning*. 3(4), 230–6.

Reid, G. (2005) *Dyslexia: A Complete Guide for Parents*. Wiley, Chichester.

Reid, G. (2003) *Dyslexia: A Practitioner's Handbook* (third edition) Wiley.

Reid, G. (2001) 'Specialist teacher training in the UK issues, considerations and future directions' in Morag Hunter-Carsch (ed.) *Dyslexia: A Psycho-social Perspective*. Whurr Publications, London.

Reid, G. (2001) 'Dyslexia, Metacognition and Learning Styles' in G. Shiel and U. Ni Dhalaigh (eds) *Reading Matters: A Fresh Start*. Reading Association of Ireland/National Reading Initiative, Dublin.

Reid, G. and Given, B. (2000) 'Learning Styles', *BDA Handbook 2000*. BDA, Reading.

Richardson, A. J. (2002) 'Dyslexia, Dyspraxia and ADHD – Can Nutrition Help?' Paper presented at Education Conference Durham County Council. June 2002.

Russell, S. (1993 & 2000) *Phonic Code Cracker*. Jordanhill College Publications, Glasgow.

Sayles, A. (2001) Paper presented at the Dyslexia Association of Ireland National Conference. University College, Dublin.

Scottish Executive (2002) 'Raising attainment of pupils with special educational needs' *Interchange*, 67:5.

Shiel, G. (2002) 'Literacy standards and factors affecting literacy: what national and international assessments tell us' in G. Reid and J. Wearmouth (eds), *Dyslexia and Literacy: Theory and Practice*. Wiley.

Silver, L. (2001) Controversial Therapies – Perspectives Vol. 27, No. 3 pp. 1, 4. *The International Dyslexia Association*, Baltimore, MD, USA.

Singleton, C. H. (2002) 'Dyslexia: Cognitive Factors and Implications for Literacy' in G. Reid and J. Wearmouth (eds) *Dyslexia and Literacy: Theory and Practice*. Wiley, Chichester.

Singleton, C. H., Horne, J. K. and Thomas, K. V. (1999) Computerised Baseline Assessment of Literacy. *Journal of Research in Reading* 22, 67–80.

Snowling, M. J. (2000) *Dyslexia* (second edition). Blackwell, Oxford.

Task Force on Dyslexia (2001) Report – Dublin: Government Publications. Available online at http://www.irlgov.ie/educ/pub.htm.

Task Group Report (2002) Task Group Report Government of Northern Ireland. Belfast, Northern Ireland.

Tod, J., Castle, F. and Blamires, M. (1998) *Implementing Effective Practice*. David Fulton Publishers, London.

Tod, J. and Fairman, A. (2001) 'Individualised learning in a group setting' in L. Peer and G. Reid (eds) *Dyslexia – Successful Inclusion in the Secondary School*. David Fulton Publishers, London.

Topping, K. J. (1996) 'Parents and peers as tutors for dyslexic children' in G. Reid (ed.), *Dimensions of Dyslexia, Vol. 2 Literacy, Language and Learning*, Moray House Publications, Edinburgh.

Topping, K. J. (2002) 'Paired Thinking, developing thinking skills through structured interaction with peers, parents and volunteers' in G. Reid and J. Wearmouth (eds) *Dyslexia and Literacy: Theory and Practice*. Wiley.

Tunmer, W. E. and Chapman, J. (1996) 'A developmental model of dyslexia. Can the construct be saved?' *Dyslexia*, 2(3), pp. 179–89.

Ulmer, C. and Timothy, M. (2001) How does alternative assessment affect teachers' practice? Two years later. Paper presented at the 12th European Conference on Reading, Dublin, Ireland, 1–4th July 2001.

Usmani, K. (1999) 'The influence of racism and cultural bias in the assessment of bilingual children'. *Educational and Child Psychology*, 16.3, pp. 44–54.

Viall, J. T. (2000) 'High Stakes Assessment' in *Perspectives* (Summer 2000 issue) Vol. 26, No. 26, p. 3. International Dyslexia Association, Baltimore.

Wearmouth, J. (2001) 'Inclusion – Changing the Variables' in L. Peer and G. Reid (eds) *Dyslexia – Successful Inclusion in the Secondary School*. David Fulton Publishers, London.

Wearmouth, J. and Reid, G. (2002) 'Issues for Assessment and Planning of Teaching and learning' in G. Reid and J. Wearmouth (eds) *Dyslexia and Literacy: Theory and Practice*. Wiley.

Wearmouth, J., Soler, J. and Reid, G. (2002) *Meeting Difficulties in Literacy Development*. Routledge/Falmer.

Weedon, C. and Reid, G. (2001) *Listening and Literacy Index*. Hodder and Stoughton, London.

Weedon, C. and Reid, G. (2003) *Special Needs Assessment Portfolio*. Hodder and Stoughton, London.

Wendon, L. (1993) 'Literacy for early childhood: learning from the learners'. *Early Child Development and Care*, pp. 86, 11–12.

West, T. G. (1991, second edition 1997) *In the Mind's Eye: Visual Thinkers, Gifted People with Learning Difficulties, Computer Images and the Ironies of Creativity*. Prometheus Books, Buffalo, NY.

Williams, F. and Lewis, J. (2001) 'Geography and Dyslexia' in L. Peer and G. Reid (eds) *Dyslexia – Successful Inclusion in the Secondary School*. David Fulton Publishers, London.

Wilson, J. and Frederickson, N. (1995) 'Phonological awareness training: an evaluation'; *Educational and Child Psychology*, 12(1), pp. 68–79.

Wray, D. (1994) *Literacy and Awareness*. Hodder & Stoughton, London.

Wray, D. (2002) 'Metacognition and Literacy' in G. Reid and J. Wearmouth (eds) *Dyslexia and Literacy: Theory and Practice*. Wiley.

Wolf, M. and O'Brien, B. (2001) 'On issues of time, fluency and intervention' in A. Fawcett (ed.) *Dyslexia: Theory and Good Practice*. Whurr Publications, London.

Printed in the United Kingdom
by Lightning Source UK Ltd.
120208UK00006B/11